PIONEER
YOUR
PIVOT

A SURVIVAL KIT
FOR CAREER CROSSROADS

MIKE YEH

Cover Designer: Bukovero, bukovero.com
Interior Formatting: Edge of Water Designs

ISBNs:
Hardcover - 979-8-9988100-1-5
Paperback - 979-8-9988100-0-8
eBook - 979-8-9988100-2-2

Publisher: Yx3

DEDICATION

To Joe and Lynda,
My loving parents who always encouraged
me to create a path that's truly my own.

TABLE OF CONTENTS

INTRODUCTION

In 2024, the U.S. Bureau of Labor Statistics reported that Americans change jobs an average of nine times between the ages of 18 and 36.[1] That's a new position every two years. It's unclear from the report whether they are including internships, but if they are, then I'd say those numbers are about right.

After graduating from college, I was an intern at Nike, held two positions at Zappos (Amazon), and then moved on to Gap, where I worked a few years until taking a break to get a master's degree. I was then an intern at Mattel, after which they hired me and later promoted me. And now I'm with Yelp. In all, I've held eight different jobs so far in my adult life.

Just mentioning the number "eight" doesn't give you the full story, though. During that timeframe, I also made a complete career switch. I changed job functions, going from inventory analyst to product marketer, then switched business industry sectors from retail to tech.

In other words, I know from firsthand experience that while changing jobs can be difficult, making a complete career switch puts you in a whole other stratosphere of difficulty.

So why do it? Why change job functions or industries?

---

[1] Bureau of Labor Statistics, U.S. Department of Labor, "People born between 1980 and 1984 held an average of 9.0 jobs from ages 18 through 36," June 26, 2024. https://www.bls.gov/opub/ted/2024/people-born-between-1980-and-1984-held-an-average-of-9-0-jobs-from-ages-18-through-36.htm.

There are too many reasons to list them all, but here's a quick summary: better money, better opportunities for career development, and better chances to expand intellectually. There's also the interest and intrigue factor, the inspired feeling of following your bliss and discovering your life's purpose and passion. And finally, sometimes you do it simply because you landed the job you thought you always wanted in a particular industry that resonated with you, only to discover a few years later that you want to do something else.

I've experienced all of the above. And, yes, making the switch was worth it. Every. Time.

What Are *Your* Plans?

When you first started your career, you probably searched for a position doing something you always thought you wanted to do. So you landed a particular job within a particular industry, and all went well for a while. You settled in and things became routine. You were doing fine, but that's when something interesting happens.

You start to notice that many of your peers are getting new jobs or moving to bigger companies. They seem to have better titles, too.

From the outside, you don't know what's really going on with them. You don't know if that "VP" in bold letters under their name on LinkedIn is truly an elevated position or just a fancy title. But that unknown doesn't seem to matter. An anxiety sets in.

Suddenly, it seems everywhere you go, you're discovering more and more people are ahead of you. Career changes are announced on social media with great enthusiasm. You attend a class reunion, and everyone but you seems to be talking about their fabulous new gig in fields you never even knew they were interested in. You're tailgating at a football game, and all your friends are talking about the great things they're doing *in their new jobs*. Jobs that are in totally different industries from where they used to be.

There's an aura of glamor about most of it. You can't help but wonder if maybe you could make a switch, too. Maybe make more money. Maybe find an opportunity to work on something new, something rewarding. Maybe even accelerate your career. Or maybe you just want to try something different.

It can't be that hard to make a switch, right? After all, everyone else is doing it. The idea lights up something within you, so you start pursuing open positions in new functions or industries. You send in some resumes. You wait to hear back.

You wait some more.

And wait some more.

Maybe you get invited to an interview … but nothing happens after that.

You feel as if you've just wasted your time and energy, possibly even some money. Even worse, your self-esteem might take a hit because you've allowed yourself to believe in what appears to be false hopes.

I'm here to tell you that this doesn't have to be your story. It *is* possible to pivot and make a career switch, regardless of where you're starting from. However, you have to go into it with the right mindset, because you will face rejection (possibly more than once), and you must be willing to put in a little (or a lot of) hard work. If you're ready and willing to do that work, though, then this book is for you.

Who Am I?

At this point, you may be wondering what you can learn from me; specifically, about switching your career. So let me tell you a little about myself.

I immigrated to America when I was just 13 years old. Like my parents, I had the American dream: I wanted a better life than what was possible for me in my home country. And I can honestly say that I achieved it. As my resume proves, I had the freedom to make a career choice … and then another career choice. Not only have I worked for Fortune 500 companies and other large organizations, but I've also been successful at switching between them, even when I've moved to an entirely different industry.

But what makes my vantage point unique is that I haven't just gone through the process of switching careers. I've also been a hiring manager.

So I've had the opportunity to sit on the other side of the desk and be a part of the decision-making process on whether or not a potential candidate would be hired.

By bringing both parts of my background—the career switcher and the career decision-maker—to this book, I can shed some light on how to make the switch and what you can expect as you go through that process. I can also explain the factors taken into consideration by the hiring side. My goal is that, armed with this information, your career-pivot journey will be shorter and have fewer twists and turns than most people's experiences.

It Is a Tough Process

Sure, there are probably some cases where people get very fortunate and happen to be in the right place at the right time, and *boom*! They get a new dream job with relative ease. For the rest of us, though, it's a challenging process. And it can take a long time.

How long, exactly? Well, obviously it can vary, but in my experience, I've found that 6 to 12 months is a good average.

Did you just balk at the idea of 6 to 12 months? If you feel you don't have that kind of time—perhaps you are in a position where your company announced massive layoffs, or is filing for bankruptcy, or some other urgent event—and you need to find a new job now, then find one! That should be your priority: Get your livelihood secured first. Once you do that, if you still want to switch functions or industries, then pick up this book again.

Really, having the ability to search for a dream job is a luxury—especially when you acknowledge that dream job may be a moving target! This is not a process to make sure you have food on the table. It's a process for when your basic needs are met and you have the time to devote to it.

To make sure you use that time wisely, we'll first explore why it's so hard to make a change. That is what the first part of this book will focus on. You'll start out by understanding that whenever you want to switch job functions or industries, there will be a few gaps in your knowledge that will prevent you from being an ideal candidate.

Some of those gaps will be in the world of language. Do you know the lingo? The acronyms? The industry jargon? Learning about them and mastering their use may be integral for advancing beyond the first interview, so we'll discuss how to close that gap.

Depending on how big of a transition you intend to make with your career switch, there may be a huge experience gap you'll need to bridge, too. To do that, the answer isn't necessarily going back to college and becoming an intern to work your way up. There are workarounds that you can take and other methodologies that will shorten the size of your gap—or simply offset it. It's very possible to be hired in a new company where your new team expects you to have a larger learning curve than if they'd hired someone whom they could "plug and play" in that position. The key is making sure they know you're worth it in the interview, and we'll discuss how to make that happen.

Bridging gaps and honing your interview skills can take a toll on your psyche, especially when rejections start piling up. On top of that, you may feel as if you are alone on your journey—because, really, you are. You are the one researching, learning, interviewing, and doing everything else that goes along with it by yourself. Being able to keep your spirits up as you navigate the ups and downs of career switching will prove invaluable. So we'll talk about ways to learn to support yourself as you go through the process.

One thing that will increase your resilience is to keep in mind that hiring decisions are never personal. I'll be giving you an overview of what it's like on the other side of the hiring desk, which will help you understand why hiring someone who is *not* a plug-and-play candidate is a risky move for a hiring manager.

Not only will this help to take the sting out of rejections, but also, by understanding what hiring teams are looking for, you'll learn about ways to accommodate them, which will position you to look like a less risky option.

In short, the first half of the book will cover how to get in the right mindset and prepare yourself to make a career switch.

Then, in the second part of the book, you'll get a little more hands-on.

Part 2 will be focused on the how-to-do-it details of career switching. We'll begin by going through the process of getting clarity on your "why." Switching may not be the only solution for you. Depending on what you really want, you may have other options to get to where you want to go. While those other solutions will not be fully addressed in this book, through this exercise, you will do a little self-exploration to get to the "why" behind your career switch. Knowing that why will help you maintain your momentum when times get tough.

To be completely honest, if you're changing careers just because that's what all your peers are doing and you're feeling as if you're falling behind, then going through the rest of this book will not be in your best interest. If your heart is not completely committed to changing jobs, then you'd be better off doing something like going out to enjoy a birthday party than intensely preparing for an interview. And that is okay! Always remember, life is an amazing gift, and we all have a limited time to enjoy it. If a career switch is not the top priority for you, then by all means, focus on what is and on what will bring you joy.

If it is a top priority, if it is something you think will bring immense pleasure to your life, then continue reading … and do the frameworks!

To help you with this, you'll find a couple of frameworks in Part 2. The first will help you get to the ultimate why of your career hunt. The second framework will help you to identify your specific knowledge gaps for the specific positions that you want. You'll then determine how to fill them or work around them.

We'll also talk about prioritization here, because it's important to understand there is a need to prioritize your actions based on what's going to yield the biggest and best results. You can search the internet, ask ChatGPT, listen to podcasts, read books, or find other ways to gather information and guidance, but there are only a few core things that are absolutely worth your time and effort. It's really hard to curate what you truly need to do and how to do it. So, instead of trying to throw 10 different spaghetti plates against the wall to see which ones will stick, you'll realize that not all noodles are created equal, and if you stick to the core ones presented, you won't need the rest.

Once the frameworks are complete and the job hunt is on, you may find yourself in a position where you're not sure whether you should take a job that is offered to you. So we'll discuss revising your why and even how your "whys" can change throughout the tenure of your career.

Then we'll end the book with everything you need to know (and possibly more) to rock your interviews. You'll learn an assortment of hints and tips to use in your preparation before interviews as well as when you're in the room where the decision-making happens.

"Clarity is Power,"[2] Tony Robbins says, which is really the main goal of this book: to provide clarity on what to expect, how you can set yourself up for success, and how to take the steps necessary to achieve a career transition.

You are already armed with a core requirement: a desire to change and a willingness to learn what to do. It's time to identify what it is you truly want to do, what you feel compelled to do, or even what you need to do. And then do it!

It's the greatest feeling in the world! Yes, you worked your tail off to chase after it, but you grow so very much as a result. That sense of pride from taking control of your own destiny is something you'll never shake. On top of that, you'll get to enjoy the fruit of all your labor when you reach the finish line: You'll experience the job you truly want.

Are you ready?

---

2   Tony Robbins, Unleash the Power Within, live event, March 21–24, 2024.

PART 1

WHY IT'S HARD TO MAKE THE CHANGE

CHAPTER 1

LEARNING A NEW LANGUAGE

When I worked in product marketing at Mattel, my job was basically to learn what the customers' needs or wants were and translate them for the product development team. I would then lead the product creation process and market the team's finished product back to the consumer.

At that time, the toy market was beginning to grapple with the very real impact of children becoming digitally literate at younger and younger ages. They were aging out of traditional toys and discovering new electronic ones at younger ages than ever before. While yes, that meant toy companies had the opportunity to develop electronic toys for them, it also meant that the lifespan of the analog ones was shrinking.

To counter that growing problem, Mattel began to explore new ways to bridge digital literacy to traditional toys in an effort to extend a child's interest in playing with them. I had the good fortune of being on the team tasked with developing that solution for Hot Wheels cars. It was very exciting for me.

My role as product marketer was basically the same; however, I now had the opportunity to work directly with hardware, software, and firmware engineers, as well as with game designers and others in the gaming studio sphere. It was my first direct exposure to working in the tech world, and I found it all to be very exciting. The experience allowed me to develop new mental muscles that I didn't even know were a possibility prior to the project. And being on the leading edge of a potential new product gave me a firsthand glimpse into the endless possibilities of technology, which was both fascinating and daunting.

I was so intrigued by everything I was learning. And with the idea that there would always be so much more to learn in the tech space, I may have been more eager than the rest of the team was anticipating. I peppered the engineers with more questions than were really needed, some that even went beyond the scope of the projects.

After we brought the product to market, I realized I'd developed a taste for the tech space, and I wanted more. I also realized that if I worked for a tech company, I would have more possibilities to expand in my job function than I would in the consumer products industry I was in. Further, I also realized I could expand financially, too, because the tech industry tends to pay better than the traditional product industry. So it seemed to me, at that time, I should make the leap from the retail toy industry to the tech one.

That leap was a bit bigger than I was able to jump at that time. Where I fell short was not where I had first expected. It wasn't my lack of tech skills that kept me at Mattel a little while longer; it was my language skills.

Talking Shop

I saw a position open up at Meta. They were looking for a product marketer for their new video-calling device. If you'd asked me about the job when I found the opening, I would have said it was the right job at the right time, and I was the right candidate for it for a number of reasons.

First, product marketing was relatively new as a career path. As such, the job's definition and description varied across companies, which meant the role offered numerous opportunities to grow your skill set and learn new ways of thinking. It also meant that it was a great job to have when you wanted to move from one industry to another. The basic core function I described earlier is always the same, but companies expect the position to have a bit of a learning curve for anyone they hire since the expectations are probably different from other companies.

Second, the job checked off a number of boxes to make it sound like a great opportunity for me. It was in the tech space—an area where I wanted to move my career into—and the product resonated with something in me.

Whenever I consider a new job, I always make sure it's something that I can relate to. If I can imagine myself being the user, then being that bridge between the user and the solution feels possible, even natural. The position at Meta was for their Portal video-calling device—something that would allow people to connect via video through Facebook Messenger. My parents don't live in the States—they live in Asia—and I called them regularly through Facebook Messenger, so being on a team that was designing ways to make video calls with them that much easier was something I knew I could be passionate about.

Third was the retail aspect of the product. It was possible to buy the product on Facebook, but people could also get it at Best Buy, Target, or other retail stores. Because I was already familiar with retail, I expected to be able to resell my experience in that space as a bridge to the tech world.

The truth is the job at Meta checked a lot of boxes and would have been my dream job if I'd been fully aware of what my dream job would entail. That is, if I'd done the framework exercises you'll discover later in this book. At that time, I hadn't invented the framework, so I didn't see the position as the ultimate job for me. It was more hardware-oriented than software, so instead I saw it as a potential interim step.

Similarly, when thinking about your current job and the job you ultimately want, you might realize you'll need to take on a few other jobs in between. Few people (if any) can make the jump from medical device sales to investment banker without creating stepping stones of jobs in between.

Likewise, multiple steps (meaning other jobs) may be between where you are and where you want to be. The Portal project at Meta seemed like such a position for me. I knew that if I could step between industries while keeping the same job function as a product marketer, it would be my entry into the tech world, where I'd be able to learn and get the experience necessary to eventually get the job I really wanted.

However, that didn't matter in the end.

I had made it through an interview with the recruiter and was on my first call with the hiring manager. I went into the call feeling totally prepared. This was the call where they'd get to know who I was, discover the range of my skill set, and start learning about my potential for the position. I expected questions like "Tell me about a time when you really advocated or pushed for an idea that was not supported by the rest of the team," and "Tell me about a time when you were new on the job and had a lot to learn," or "How do you deal with conflict?"

I'd done my homework and knew that these types of behavior questions would be lobbed at me during that first-round interview, so I had created answers for each one. Additionally, I researched other questions that are often asked in that line of work, and I even read Meta's earnings announcements to know what their strategy was. I knew I wouldn't be expected to know the internal jargon specific to their company, but I would be expected to understand the basic ideas of what they were doing and some of the key terms that are used throughout the tech world.

Again, I was prepared. I knew it was my job going into the interview to connect whatever dots I could from what I had done in the past to what this new potential position would require of me.

Then I was asked, "How would you price a product?"

Now, I had experience in pricing products … in the retail world. So I gave a very detailed answer on how I would do it. A very detailed answer that was based on selling to a buyer working with a retail outlet who would place my product on their shelves for people to purchase.

Unfortunately, on that question, I failed to connect some very important dots. The question was actually about how to research pricing for a product. In the tech world, a heavy emphasis is placed on customer research and data gathering. The data, then, is what drives the decision on price point. Tech companies often sell directly to consumers, and new technology often has more flexibility in pricing. So, to price a product in the tech world, you rely on surveying consumers to determine how much they'd be willing to pay for a product, then calculate how to control the price to optimize profit.

That's a different scenario than what I'd experienced at Mattel, a company that works with retail buyers in order to get traditional products on store shelves. Since these traditional products are all similar across brands, the pricing decisions for those retail products are determined heavily by data built out of competitor pricing, retailer margin, etc. Unfortunately for me, I didn't realize my interviewer was expecting a totally different pricing strategy than the one I gave.

Once I finished my answer, I faced a good five long seconds of silence.

As you will learn later, it wasn't the first time I had to sit through such an awkward silence, so I knew it was not a good sign.

The manager recovered and asked me for more details. She asked several questions that, in hindsight, were probably her way of trying to get me to give her the right answer. Unfortunately, her questions only confused me—I couldn't figure out why she was even asking about pricing! What other way of pricing was there?

Eventually, she gave up and moved on to other questions. I could feel the energy shift in the call and knew not to expect another interview.

A few weeks later, at dinner with my friend Morgan from business school—a friend who happens to work at tech giant PayPal—we talked about my interview. Finally, the dots were connected!

"Dude," Morgan said. "You completely missed the point of that question! You forgot what Professor Smith taught us about conjoint analysis, of running different data models and price points."

The feedback was spot on. I had been stuck in the language of Mattel, of analog products and retail pricing structures. I had given a correct answer … for *my* industry. We were speaking different languages, and my interpretation had led to me translating the question completely inaccurately.

Learning a New Tongue

Whatever industry you are in, there are specific ways of doing things (like pricing) that, for the most part, are customary to that industry. Likewise, there will be expectations and experiences that define what the industry does, which means it has a unique language. Even if one industry shares a job function with another, they will differ in word usage and twists of phrases.

So, part of the preparation for a career change requires you to do some research to find out what it is that you don't know. You have to learn enough of the industry's language to make the person interviewing you realize you have enough baseline knowledge to be safe to move to the next round of interviews. If you do that, then you would do better than me in that Meta interview; you would understand the intent of their questions and provide an answer that would make sense to them.

Remember, this is *your* responsibility! After I botched that interview, I complained to my parents about the manager who interviewed me. I blamed it on her. "What kind of question is that?! She's working at Facebook, and she doesn't even know how things work!" But it was me. I wasn't fluent in the language she spoke.

To be fluent in another industry's language means that you understand what the person sitting across from you (or on the other end of the phone call) is looking for and why they are asking you a specific question. The key is in the listening part of language—understanding what is being asked, not just what the meaning of the word being spoken is.

The other side of fluency is being able to return your communication in a way that clearly explains your experience and answers the question the interviewer asks. It means you can connect the dots between your experience and what they are looking for, even if you've never worked in that industry before.

One way to become fluent is to start educating yourself with content. After realizing I needed to become fluent in the tech space, I went on YouTube to listen to mock interviews and watch people debrief and discuss their application processes. I also took classes from LinkedIn Learning. Every industry is different, and everyone's budget is different, but you have numerous options available to you. There are numerous books you can read, podcasts you can listen to, newsletters to sign up for ... the list goes on and on. The point is to look for and immerse yourself in content that will provide you with the language you need to feel comfortable in interviews.

You can also learn from your mistakes (and your wins). If you have interviews over Zoom, for example, you can ask the interviewer if it's permissible for you to record the meeting—or, if it's already recorded, ask for a copy of it. Then go back and listen to yourself, see where you got caught up, and find ways to improve. I did this frequently in my subsequent interviews. I would listen to the question and pause to think about what the person was asking. Then I'd listen to my answer to see if I truly answered the question.

I would also study and dissect the transcripts from those interviews, which helped me discover how the questions could be asked and answered from different perspectives or with different intents. Once I got a sense of what a question *really* meant versus how I originally interpreted it, I would go back and review my answer and determine how I could have said it differently or better or been more concise.

In other words, I learned the language and applied it to my answers. There were times when I'd rewrite an answer 20 or 30 times! Okay, yes, that might have been a little overkill, but I could guarantee that the next time that question came up in an interview, my fluency rate had improved so much I was able to answer it in ways that felt natural to me.

Mock interviews can also be very helpful for you to learn industry fluency. Ask someone to play the role of the interviewer for you. If you don't have a willing candidate, interview yourself. Ask yourself questions and answer them, recording the whole process so you can listen, rate yourself, and find ways to improve.

Another tactic is to leverage your network. Ask someone you know who works in the industry if they'd have a 15-minute informational call with you. Once you're on that call with them, ask them how they would respond to the interview questions. This is a great way to figure out if you truly understand the questions that are being asked in the interviews.

One thing to keep in mind is that there is no one right place to start. Becoming fluent in another industry's language is like learning a real foreign language. You often learn words, especially at the beginning of your education, that you don't use frequently, if at all. However, if you keep speaking that language, at some point every word you learn will be useful. That happened to me when I learned English. My first English word was *apple*, which isn't a word that I used on a regular basis. In fact, I did not need to know *apple* until about a year later when I was in a supermarket, where I used it correctly.

The same situation will happen with you as you learn an industry-specific language. Don't discount any terms or phrases. You just never know when you'll find yourself needing to use them.

Learning a new language will be easier for you if you find a mentor who is willing to help you. As you read this book, you'll discover that finding a mentor is a theme I touch on repeatedly. That's because the insight and wisdom of a mentor is hard to beat. Frankly, I think one of the few good reasons for networking is to find such a mentor. But, if worse comes to worst and you can't find someone through networking, you can always hire a mentor or coach, should you have the budget for it. If you go that route, though, make sure that it pays off. You need to be sure you find somebody who speaks the right industry language fluently, but also someone who, as you go through the process of finding a new job, will help prevent you from going in the wrong direction.

Yes, becoming fluent can monopolize all your spare time. It may take so much energy that you'll question whether the pivot is worth it. That is why it is so important to be clear on your *why* for finding a new job. We'll cover that later in Part 2 of the book. For now, just keep in mind: Changing job functions or industries will require more from you than applying for a similar job to what you have now.

Becoming Fluent

After I recovered from my interviewing gaff with Meta, I learned what I needed to do for the next interview. I also understood that if I waited until

I knew everything possible about an industry, I'd probably never apply for another job.

The point is to recognize there may be a language gap that could impair your ability to communicate with the company you're interviewing with. Once you recognize there is a potential gap there, then you can find a way to fill it well enough that you can successfully answer the questions your interviewer asks. By gaining this kind of fluency, the hiring team will know you understand their questions, and they will know what you intend to convey. However, you have to be realistic. You will always have more to learn, and you will not ever be able to learn everything prior to your next interview.

Read that last sentence again.

The important thing is that you recognize there is a language gap and do whatever you can to close it. That's different from getting the equivalent of another college degree by learning everything possible. Granted, it's hard to be at peace with accepting you don't know what you don't know. But you never will.

I learned that lesson the hard way. I had interned at Nike, and my dream job (at that time) was to return to Nike. That was before I learned how to prepare for interviews, so I followed the age-old advice of keeping my connections open. Every other month, I'd call James, a coworker during my internship at Nike, to check in on the projects he was working on and maintain my understanding of the strategic direction of the company. My belief at the time was that when there would be an opening on his team, I'd be one step ahead of the other candidates by knowing the strategic direction of the company. I also figured that by maintaining my connection with him, I'd be the first person he'd think of for the job.

It's possible that strategy would have worked—*if* I'd spent some time learning the language that would be required of me as a team member. Instead, when James was talking about a strategy during one of our update calls, he said a word I didn't understand. He mentioned creating a "SKU" for a product. Three or four minutes later, I was even more confused and finally mustered up the courage to interrupt him to ask, "What does 'SKU' mean?"

He'd mentioned it several times by then, but the context clues didn't fill it in for me.

That was the first time I experienced an awkward silence over the phone. James is probably one of the nicest people I know, though, and he took the time to define what a SKU was and provided a use case for it. He went on to explain how it enabled several different processes to work within the inventory system. We continued our conversation, but I could sense I had damaged my reputation instead of maintaining my position at the top of the list of potential candidates.

Now I realize that not understanding what a SKU was meant that I lacked a basic piece of knowledge that I needed if I was ever to work in any kind of product or retail environment (and I now understand it well!). But I didn't know it then. If I had just gone to the library and picked up a book on retail, I'd have known what a SKU was. Certainly, if I'd relied on Google, YouTube, Wikipedia, or any number of free resources to research the retail space that Nike is in, I'd have been better prepared. But that wasn't the approach I took then, because I didn't know what I didn't know, and didn't think to look for it.

And again: That. Is. Okay. You will *never* know what you don't know. The point is to recognize just that: Since there is an inevitable gap in your knowledge, you will need to learn as much as possible about the industry or job function you are wanting to move into, while still accepting that you will never know everything.

While I had prepared myself for the conversations between James and me, I never really tried to evolve myself in a way where I would better understand the industry, the business, and my dream job company. If I had kept educating myself, I would have learned at least the basic information, such as what a SKU was, because I would have picked up on the retail language.

I also would have discovered more things that I didn't know because there wasn't just a language gap. Any time you want to change industries or functions, there will be an experiential gap in addition to the language one. Because even if you learn to speak the same language, you will still not have the 10 years of experience that another potential candidate for that position will have. However, if you are able to shorten that experiential gap by compensating with knowledge, then you will improve your odds of landing that dream job. So let's look at ways to mind that gap next.

CHAPTER 2

MINDING THE GAP

The gap I had to shorten to land my job with Mattel was actually much broader than just a language gap. Essentially, the position would be my first in a marketing role, which was the kind of job I'd wanted since I'd started college.

In fact, when I first graduated college, I had my heart set on a marketing career. But, because I graduated shortly after the 2008 financial crisis, getting any kind of job was difficult. I didn't have the luxury of applying only for marketing positions. Instead, I had to take the first job that was made available to me, which happened to be in merchandise planning at Zappos—a position that my product management internship with Nike helped me achieve. Subsequently, a couple of years later, I moved into inventory planning at Gap.

I did wind up enjoying what I was doing, and I appreciated everything I learned during my time at Nike, Zappos, and then at Gap. However, my interest in marketing never waned. I still felt like it was something I wanted to try. Additionally, my entire work tenure had been in the retail industry, and I was intrigued by the idea of working in entertainment or possibly even in the tech space.

So, after taking a break to go back to school for my MBA, I decided to focus on getting a job in marketing, hopefully in an entertainment or tech company.

While I knew where I wanted to focus, after I started my job hunt and rejections began coming in, I started to feel a bit demoralized. It seemed no one wanted to interview me, and if they did, they didn't want a second interview. When I was near the point of giving up and returning to an inventory position for a retail company, I called my sister, seeking commiseration about my situation.

As soon as she answered, I started complaining about how hard it was, about how unfair it seemed that I wasn't even getting beyond a first interview. It seemed to me that if those companies would just give me a chance in a second interview, then I would have a better chance at proving myself.

"Stop!" my sister eventually cut me off. "Let's think about this differently."

"What do you mean?"

"I mean, think about it like this: To get into business school, you had to take a standard exam before the school would interview you, right?"

"Right."

"Then, only after that interview could they decide whether they would offer you a spot in the school, right?"

"Right. So?" I was getting impatient. My sister is usually much wiser and smarter than me, but it didn't seem like she was of much help that day.

"So my point is, those 'first-round' interviews are not really the first ones for everyone. Your competition has already gone through rigorous exams and interviews to get into MBA programs, just like you've done. So everyone you're competing with has already proven that they are capable, because they got a seat in one of those programs. Really, you could say these interviews are like second- or even third-round ones, which means they are super competitive.

"Also, you're not looking at entry-level positions. You're looking at positions in a later stage of your career than where you were before. That means you and the other applicants are expected to have strong experience or deep knowledge. Sure, you have marketing classes under your belt, but you're competing against people who have passed the standard exam and interview to get into business school as well as having more experience in the field than you do."

She was right. I was looking at Fortune 500 companies, where a lot of people want to work and where there were very few jobs. I'd completely underestimated the level of competition I'd be up against. I was in a highly competitive landscape. Of course it would be hard!

My sister gave me some great advice that day, but what was most helpful was that she made me realize I hadn't done enough to prepare for my interviews. I may have learned the language of marketing in some of the classes I took while earning my MBA, but there was still a gap in my knowledge and experience, particularly regarding the positions I was looking at with entertainment companies. I wasn't just switching jobs—going from one position to a similar one in a similar company. I was switching job functions *and* hoping to make an industry switch as well. Meanwhile, I was competing with people who had deep marketing experience and who knew the industry very well.

Was it even possible to make a career switch like that? It almost sounded like a catch-22: In order to be competitive with other applicants, I'd need to know the language and have the experience they did—but I couldn't acquire either without having worked in those jobs in that industry.

The good news is, it is possible to make such a switch. You can acquire the knowledge you need to shorten the gap, which will make you competitive against others who have already had the job you want. And you can do things to make you such an attractive candidate that the hiring team will give you a pass for having that gap. The first thing you have to do, though, is understand what kind of switch you are making.

The Kind of Switch Matters

Knowing what kind of switch you want to make matters. The challenges facing you will depend on what, exactly, will be different in your career: How many changes do you intend to make, and what kind will they be? Being able to answer those questions will help you set the proper expectations for your road ahead. Broadly speaking, there are three different kinds of switches you can make:

1. **Industry-only Switch.** When you realize you love what you're doing, but the industry you're working in feels lackluster to you, you may want to make an industry-only change. Here, you'll find a new position doing what you're doing now, but in an industry that you find more appealing. The gaps you will have to bridge will mostly be about your industry knowledge.

2. **Function-only Switch.** Here you want to make a career switch to do something different, but stay in the same field. Examples of this kind of switch include moving from being in sales with a retail company to being in human resources for another retail company. Bridging gaps here will focus on your job skills.

3. **Industry and Function Switch.** This is when you want to do both: find a position that has a different job function *and* is in a different industry compared to where you are now. If this is your goal, you can expect that it will be a little harder to bridge the gaps before you, because you will have to fill in both industry knowledge and job skills.

To further clarify what a function-only or industry-only switch looks like, we'll say that if you have 80 percent of the skills required in your prospective position's job description, then you're not really switching functions. Similarly, if your current industry shares 80 percent of the characteristics that the other company's industry has, then you're not really making an industry switch.

It's easier to make a function-only or industry-only switch than to do both because, as mentioned above, there are fewer gaps that you need to fill. However, industry and function switches are definitely possible.

The key to being successful with any type of switch is in knowing where you are starting in relation to where you want to end. To use a Formula One analogy: If you are starting in P15 (position 15 at the starting line), you have a larger gap to overcome than if you are starting in P1 (the first position at the starting line). It is important to recognize whatever position you are in because it is only by acknowledging how far you need to go that you will know what you need to do to get there.

There's No Such Thing as "Overprepared"

Once you know what your starting position is, you can prepare to make up for the gap between you and the people in P1 competing against you. That means you begin doing everything you can to be prepared for the interviews. How do you do that?

You start by researching what the company is doing, what their goals are, and what possible issues are threatening to impede their progress toward their goals. You learn about their culture and their branding style. And you try to find connections between your experience to all of that.

For example, if you are going to be interviewed by Lyft, which is a public company, the first thing to do would be to read through their 10-K, which is the annual report they file with the SEC that talks about their state of business. That report discusses the direction the company wants to head in and includes all the ins and outs about how they are doing financially and how they intend to move strategically.

If you are being interviewed by a private company, they will not have to file public reports, so finding similar research on them may be harder. The "About" page on their website is always a good place to start. Of course, internet searches can help you get a better understanding, too; sometimes, you can find presentations from company execs online—even on YouTube—or information about their latest projects in the news.

Aside from gaining a thorough understanding of the specific companies, I also advise reading through industry news reports and checking to see what their competitors are up to. Go through your contacts: Do you know anyone who works at those companies, or do they know someone? Speak with those people to learn about the culture of the company and any other insights they can share.

What you do with all this information is fill in the gaps of your knowledge and background. You absorb the information as much as possible, so when you're in the interview you can tailor your answers to their questions through the lens of what you've learned. The ultimate goal is to prove to the hiring team that you understand how their company operates, what their goals are, and what some of their challenges are.

The second part of your preparation is to research what it's like to be interviewed by the companies you're applying to. Glassdoor is a great tool to help you do this. You can read through the questions that are commonly asked by those companies and start rehearsing or preparing your own answers to them. I used to take the questions and then write and rewrite my answers, incorporating what I learned from my research until I felt they were fully fleshed-out responses.

As you work on crafting your answers, remember that part of preparing for an interview includes thinking about how you can integrate your past experience with the role of the job you're applying for. That is one of the ways you will prove you can bridge what might appear as a gap between where you are now in your career and where you're applying to be.

Of course, you'll be doing more than just interviewing. Eventually, as you go through the interview process, you will be tested in terms of how you think and interact with other people with a task or case question. That's especially true within the tech industry, where you will be tasked to do a project that proves you can strategically think about and present an idea in front of executives. All of the research and prep work you've done for the interview will be very helpful when it comes to these kinds of questions, often called case questions. We'll talk more about them in Chapter 9, so I won't go into too many details on them now. Just be aware that when you present your answer in these situations, you will be asked questions by panel members, who will challenge your thinking. It's stressful, but you learn a lot!

When I interviewed with Uber, after I'd made it through several rounds, I was tasked with designing an Uber service for laundry. The task sent me deep into research mode, as I had no idea what the infrastructure for such a prospect would look like, who else was out there already doing it, and how strong of a business opportunity it even was.

When I presented the case, it was before a panel of three people, one of whom was the hiring manager. The presentation went well, but I didn't get the job. Still, I benefited from it because the hiring manager stayed on the call with me afterward to provide instant feedback, which was super helpful for all interviews going forward. However, when I interviewed with Endeavor, my experience went in a totally different direction.

It Happened Again

When I first started the process of transitioning from Mattel, I was very fortunate to land an interview with Endeavor, the business that owns WWE as well as other companies. It was an exciting interview for me because they are a huge company looking to use tech to transform the entertainment experience for their customers. It's also an entertainment company, which is one of the industries that I found appealing. They contract with many major motion picture stars, Dwayne "The Rock" Johnson among them.

At the time of my interview, they were forming a brand-new team focused on creating a digital VIP experience to offer football fans. They wanted to offer something innovative that was not another form of ticketing.

I made it so far in the interview process that I had the opportunity to be tasked on that project. In particular, I was to propose a new product that would enhance the experience of people who bought VIP tickets.

I treated the project like I was cramming for a final exam. I researched and researched and researched some more. I read books and took online courses. I did everything I could to learn as much as possible. I built a plan and then presented it to a panel of vice presidents, senior vice presidents, and managers. I gave the presentation, then I had to answer their questions.

But you know what? There was still a gap.

I presented the project to the CMO of the group and a few different vice presidents. I spoke about business opportunities and how I would measure success. I even included a few metrics that I would track. It all sounded great to me. But then the CMO asked a couple of questions.

She appreciated that I had created metrics and defined KPIs for this business component, but she wanted to see how they would work in a different scenario or alternative perspective. She asked how I would change the metrics in a different business condition, or if there were ones that I thought were still missing.

I had no idea how to answer her. All my thoughts and theories were just on paper. So I simply repeated the same thing that I'd already said. It was tough to get through. Frankly, while preparing for this book, I went back and listened to that interview. I had asked for a copy of the recording of that presentation at the time, and they were happy to share it with me. Listening to it now still hurts.

However, I learned from it. And looking back on the project, I see that it exposed that what I'd learned in academia, the theory-based concepts, differed somewhat from reality. I thought I knew what I needed to know, but now that I'm on the other side, I can see what the CMO was asking: She could foresee some of the things that could go wrong with my proposal and was looking to see how well I could pivot.

Unfortunately, at the time I didn't have the experience I do now, so I wasn't able to connect those dots for her. There was still a very large gap. To go back to the Formula One analogy, I wasn't aware of where I was in the starting lineup—in fact, I had overestimated myself. I thought I was in P8, about midway down the starting lineup. But really, I was closer to P15. I had taken for granted that my research would be enough to position me near the leader. Unfortunately, my lack of knowledge was exposed in the case question.

The good news is that, with the new understanding I gained by learning from that failed presentation, I was able to shorten my gap. I went and asked other people how they would answer the question, and I searched for articles and classes on how to address it. And the more I learned, the better I was at closing the gap. In other words, I connected the dots and made a fuller picture of who I was and what I could do on the job.

Connecting the Dots

As a hiring manager, one of the questions I've frequently asked interviewees is to tell me about a time when they took a chance and failed, or worked on a project that failed. I do this for a number of reasons. The most important one is that it's a great opportunity for the person I'm interviewing to prove to me that they find parallels between what they've done in the past with what will be expected of them in a new position with my company.

Having been in the hot seat—where I had to prove those parallels—I know how difficult it can be.

For example, when I was still at Mattel, I was interviewed by Amazon for a marketing position to bring a new service to market. I used that question to connect the dots between marketing for a toy company and marketing for a tech one. I spoke about how we wanted to collect data to get 100 percent certainty on a product prior to launching—but when we got to around 90 percent, we discovered that the trend for the product had already passed: The product was no longer needed in the marketplace. We had invested quite a bit in research and development, but there was nothing to show for it.

However, what I learned from that experience is that you never really get to 100 percent certainty, nor do you need to. You just need enough to validate your decision to move forward.

I realized I could continue to gather data—even after making a decision to launch a product—and that data would be more useful later, such as when I'd need to pivot and better address the needs of my customers. Also, you will continue to get more data after you launch, which will likewise help you improve the service for the customer going forward. So, I tied that lesson back to launching any product in any industry.

And there's more! By studying the company, I was able to take a good interview answer and make it a great one, something I did with Amazon.

I learned that one of Amazon's leadership principles is to have a bias for action. So, I also tapped into that in my answer: The experience helped me learn how to take calculated risks that could really accelerate the growth of the business, which proved I have a clear bias for action. So, with that one question, I showed that I could use a failure to achieve success further down the road, which fits nicely into how the company operates.

Don't Be Afraid to Occasionally Say, "I Don't Know"

While I was able to connect the dots between Amazon and Mattel, something that may have benefited me just as much was if, during a few interviews, I'd been brave enough to say, "I don't know." Most hiring managers realize there may be gaps in your experience and will be expecting you to have to bridge them in some way. But they need to know that *you're* aware of the gaps, too. Making up an answer on the fly or, like I did, simply repeating what you've stated before, only makes you appear unaware of what you have to learn. At times like that, it's always best to admit you don't know something, or ask for clarity.

It's always worse when people allow their interviewers to believe they know more than they do or have experience that they don't. Those people are only asking for complications to crop up later. When you say, "I don't know," it means the hiring team can trust you to be honest and transparent.

Of course, when you say, "I don't know," the next thing you should do is ask for clarity. In fact, I consider clarity questions the best ones to ask because often there will be an opportunity for you to show them you're able to connect dots between different subjects. If you're asked, "Can you explain X, Y, and Z?" and you can't but, after getting clarity, you're able to say, "Oh, so it's similar to A, B, and C that I have experienced," then in one sentence you prove to your interviewer that you are a critical thinker and can pivot. This will leave a good, lasting impression on the interviewer. They will see that you are adaptable and flexible.

So, it's always best to ask for clarity—it proves you're willing to learn more. There shouldn't be any worry about saving face here. You will most likely lose the battle by not asking the question, and by asking it, you may make it through to the next round.

Asking the questions and learning from them is just one more way to close the gap. I interviewed at DoorDash and did not get the job. Nor did I get the job at Endeavor, or at Meta, or at Amazon. But I took what I learned from asking questions and getting clarity from each of those application experiences and integrated it into my process when I applied at Yelp, my current position.

Additionally, outside of the research I did independently, I mentioned my job hunt to several other people. From that, I learned that reaching out to others can help you fill your gaps. After all, as the saying goes, we are only six degrees away from someone we want to know.

Six Degrees

In addition to reaching out to people you know who work at a company (or who know others who do) to get intel, there's another bonus to using your network to shorten your gap. And that's to find someone who can and will put in a good word for you.

As proof of concept, consider a podcast I listened to while working on this book. It was the GTM podcast on which the host, Scott, was talking to his new VP of marketing, Sophie. They were discussing how she had landed her job just a few months before the episode. She didn't start in P1, but she closed the gap quickly.

Scott mentioned that he had received calls from a number of people he knew, saying something like, "Hey, I know this person, Sophie, who might be talking to you about the VP of Marketing role. She's great." He heard similarly from people he spoke to at a conference. Subsequently, she moved forward in the lineup because all those people were folks Scott respected.

Because they were giving Sophie the stamp of approval, he felt like she was a candidate he could trust.

Something to keep in mind is that every hiring decision is a risk. Because people whom Scott personally knew or admired from afar spoke complimentarily about Sophie, it helped him to develop trust for her.

Here's the interesting thing: Sophie never asked any of those people to connect with Scott. She had merely mentioned to several people that she was applying for the role in his company, and because they knew her and liked her, they were happy to mention her in a positive light to him.

Another way to work with your network is to look for people already at the companies where you want to work and ask them if they'd mind answering a few questions for you. You can send them a message on LinkedIn, or if you're able to find their email address, approach them that way. Regardless, be direct, brief, and always respectful. Something like this will work fine: "I'm interested in coming to work at your company. Here are one or two questions. If you get a chance, could you type a quick response for me?"

When the Going Gets Tough

Whether you're going for an industry and function switch—like when I wanted to leave inventory planning at a retail company to move into a marketing job at an entertainment company—or you're changing only one area of your work—like when I wanted to move from a marketing position at a retail company to a similar position at a tech company—it's seldom an easy switch. As my story thus far illustrates, I wasn't originally prepared for how difficult it would be to make a switch. My expectations weren't in alignment with reality. But once my sister helped me realize I was competing at a much higher level than I'd originally thought, I was able to get off the couch and get working on closing the gap. She helped me get clarity on the situation by making me realize I was in a tougher race, which meant I needed to work harder.

It still took a long time, and the journey was often painful. Realizing that the things I was learning and the experiences I was gaining made me better at my day job with Mattel turned out to be something that boosted my spirits enough to encourage me to keep trying. With each interview, I would bring the concepts and other helpful information that I had discovered and integrate them into my work.

So, as I applied to Lyft, Snap, Apple, Robinhood, YouTube, Amazon, Discord, LinkedIn, Google, Uber, Shopify, Patreon, Salesforce, Grammarly, DoorDash, and another 20 million or so companies (if nothing else, I'm thorough!), I focused as much as I could on what I could learn from each interview. I had to keep my focus there because, with each one, I just felt torn apart. It usually only lasted for a little while, but sometimes it lingered for longer—like when I realized my test project was failing.

The thing is, you have to grow. So you have two options when something flawed about you is exposed: You can put it under a rug in the back of your mind and hope to never think of it again, or you can take the feedback, integrate it into what you've already learned, and use it to get better.

Knowing I was growing helped me to keep going. Knowing I was learning and applying what I was learning in my day job was a real motivator for me. The more I integrated the lessons I'd learned from all the interview attempts, the more I started finding myself solving the same problems differently at work. I'd use different approaches to manage projects more efficiently. I became a better communicator with peers and with leadership. And that, in turn, boosted my confidence when I needed it the most.

The Tough Get Confident

I realize that not everyone has sisters at the ready with good advice and lots of patience. I admit, I am lucky to have her in my corner. But even with her there, I needed to learn to support myself emotionally when making a switch.

There is a side benefit to closing the gap—you'll notice that you feel more and more confident as time goes on. As you build your knowledge base about an industry or company, you will become better able to tie your experience and knowledge to the experience and knowledge your interviewers will want you to have.

That growing confidence will be necessary, because making a career switch can be psychologically and emotionally taxing. Maintaining your confidence will be one way to support yourself, which brings us to learning tools for self-support.

Because regardless of how well you learn to prepare for your interviews, and how well you close the gap, you can at times just feel ripped apart and exhausted, only to have to do it all over again. At times it can feel as if you're a phoenix, going through the burn only to rise in the ashes for the next interview. Learning how to support yourself emotionally during this process will become crucial. Let's now look at some strategies to do just that.

CHAPTER 3

LEARNING TO SUPPORT YOURSELF

As mentioned in the previous chapter, making that initial switch to a marketing position was much harder than anything I'd anticipated. And much longer. I experienced rejection after rejection after rejection. Rejections are tough. Especially when they pile up.

And for me, the worst rejections were the ones from retail companies. I could understand why maybe an entertainment company wouldn't want to take a risk on me, but by the time I was looking for a job during my MBA studies, I had a great track record in retail. So imagine my surprise when I was rejected from other retail companies. I didn't even make it to the second round with a few of them. It was crushing, to put it mildly.

You probably already know to expect to have more than one interview. Your first will be a screening with someone from HR. If you make it through that, you'll get your initial conversation with a hiring manager. After that, there may be an opportunity for you to meet someone on the manager's team; eventually, you could even have a group interview with the whole team. In short, you'll have three interviews at a minimum, but some companies go through several more. For my position with Zappos, I went through six rounds of interviews.

Remember that call to my sister? By the time I made it, I'd already spent about four or five months getting rejected. Her advice to make myself a more competitive candidate was spot-on because when I first began, it felt like every response was an almost immediate "no." A few months in, after

I started closing the gap and making myself more competitive, I'd get an interview, sometimes two, before I'd be dropped out of the running.

While my sister never said anything to shame me, by finding myself in that position—lying on the couch feeling sorry for myself—I was embarrassed. I realized I needed to pull myself together and learn to support myself psychologically as I figured out how to shorten the gap and become competitive.

The question then became: How do you support yourself?

Release Your Ego

I like doing things for myself. I see my life as my journey, and I don't want to burden other people with my travelling needs. Because I want to do things for myself, I have a tendency to take on the onus of responsibility and carry the weight all by myself, too.

I'm sure there's a pride thing related to this: If I can do this alone, without support, then I get to say, *I did it!* On top of that, in total transparency, I admit I am a bit of a control freak. I like to have as much control over every input as I can so that I can have a bigger influence on the output.

However, now that I've switched careers twice, I can tell you that my greatest enlightenment was understanding that getting a little support actually makes me a stronger person.

While you're maintaining your current job, living your life outside of work, and learning what you need to bridge your industry or job function gaps, you're still limited by being human—there are only 24 hours in a day, after all. Your capacity doesn't expand just because your interests do. It's one thing to know that intellectually. It's another to put it into practice, because stepping aside to allow someone to support you requires getting your ego out of the way.

When I was growing up, my dad used to say, "You can't eat your ego for breakfast, lunch, or dinner." What he meant was that you can't feed or sustain yourself on ego. Thus, your ego is not the most important thing.

So as you prioritize what you can in life, you may discover, like I did, that you have to put your ego where it belongs (out of the way) to get the best results. Once you do that, you can accept that no one is good at everything and that, yes, you do need others in your corner.

Tapping into Your Network, Revisited

In the last chapter, I spoke about reaching out to others to ask for their input on what to expect when you're interviewing. To expand on that further, you can also reach out to people in your network to help you on multiple fronts.

While I was still in business school, I'd frequently visit my marketing professor during her office hours to get feedback on how I planned to answer job interview questions. If we studied something in class that was helpful, I'd bring that in.

I also knew that she had, like many of my professors, worked for a few major brands. So I'd ask her, "If you were to solve this particular problem, how would you do it based on your experience?" That would give me an idea of how she would think through the problem, which helped me hone my answer even more.

I'd also reach out to other people who had recently stood in my shoes but who had moved on to a position similar to what I wanted. For example, when I was a first-year grad student, I searched and connected with second-year students who would tell me what to expect. They also offered tips that had worked for them. It was particularly insightful when some folks who had received internships at Mattel mentioned they'd been asked case questions on the 4Ps of marketing.

Similarly, you can reach out to people who have made the kind of career switch you are attempting to leverage their experiences to shorten your gap. Ask how they'd answer particular questions. What were some of the unexpected challenges they ran into? Where and how did they fumble in interviews? What was most helpful to them as they prepared? See if anyone is willing to hold a mock interview with you, and if they do, be sure to get feedback from them about how you did and if there was something that seemed missing.

If you're still in school or if your school offers services to alumni, take advantage of their career service office. I found those resources to be extremely helpful, as they gave me the opportunity to prepare before each interview. I was even able to do several rounds of mock interviews with the career advisors who had industry experience, and then debrief afterward. Additionally, you can always find a career coach if your budget allows it.

Another resource that might surprise you is fellow job seekers. When you find people going toward the same destination as you, partner up with them. That means you'll prepare for interviews together, share information, and debrief together. Sure, there may only be one seat that you're competing for, but the overall experience will enable you both to become better and more competitive. No matter what, you'll both be improving. So there's nothing really you can lose.

When my friend Sadie and I prepared for our interviews with Apple, we'd individually read through the annual filings of Apple's 10-K, research what Tim Cook had said about the direction of the company, review the company's balance sheet, etc. Then we'd discuss it with each other: How did we interpret the information? What did we find that was interesting, important, or relevant in some way? When we landed interviews, we likewise debriefed with each other, comparing questions and answers. Seeing how she analyzed the report and answered things differently gave me an opportunity to see my own answers from a different perspective—and likewise, she could learn the same way from me.

Long story short, Sadie got that job. I didn't make it past the first round. However, I continued to help her prepare for the other interviews she went on, which I considered part of my own education as well. By doing so, I was able to define a benchmark for myself to compare and contrast my answers. Throughout the process, I learned as much as I could. We both did, really. And we both became more dynamic as candidates.

I had similar experiences with others. Because I was able to really infuse their perspectives and answers with my own, I believe that partnering up helped me to become a much better candidate as time went on.

It may seem odd to partner with someone who is competing for the same job as you, but if you are able to make a real and trusting connection with them, I promise you will benefit as much as I did. Also, because we helped push each other to become better, that shared experience wound up creating a strong bond between us, and we still have a great friendship to this day.

There is one caveat here. If you are going to partner with someone on your job hunt, you first must be willing to give before you will find people who will give back. Having a one-way relationship could be harder than doing it alone. If someone isn't fairly reciprocating, then you can't learn from each other and get better, which is the point.

Connect with Yourself

Regardless of how big your network is, repeatedly being turned down for job offers can still beat you down. As I mentioned earlier, when I was looking to make the switch into marketing, I was in graduate school. Being in an academic community gave me ample opportunity to go to football games, parties, and dinners with friends and partake in community service events or school projects with others. Those activities forced me to unplug myself. I didn't realize it at the time, but looking back, I can now see how those outside activities helped me stay fresh.

Later, when I was looking to leave Mattel for a tech company, I didn't have such easy access to other distractions. Nor was I part of a cohort of others who were also looking for new positions. I felt very alone as I applied to more than 20 companies, frequently striking out after that first conversation with HR.

Additionally, I was looking for a position when COVID restrictions had everyone hunkering in place. There was a basketball court outside my apartment building where I tried to take a break—by myself on the court, shooting baskets in a mask. But, where I lived, during the height of COVID, even doing that was discouraged. I was kicked off the court and told to get back inside. I felt as if I were imprisoned—while dealing with rejection after rejection after rejection. I filled the void of not having anything else to do when I wasn't working by completely throwing myself into doing better on my interviews.

I recorded myself while I held mock interviews with myself. I'd then listen to the recording multiple times, trying to remove myself somewhat so I could hear it from the perspective of somebody new to the interview. I'd evaluate my answers. Were they too long? Too short? Not clear enough? It felt very awkward at first, but after a while I got used to it and really learned from it because I could still find ways to optimize my answers.

Voicing my interview answers out loud, especially into a recording device, actually became another way that I was able to boost my morale. I guess it's similar to when actors or other performers go over their lines or sing when alone. The more they do that, the more confident they feel when they are auditioning with others. I noticed the same thing happening to me as I grew more confident in my interviews.

As time went on, everything I did to prepare for my interviews compounded. I began doing well enough that I started getting past first-round interviews and making it to second-round ones, then third-round. I could see myself moving up in my starting position, getting closer and closer to the front of the line. I began telling myself that if I could just push myself a little harder, I'd make it to P1 and land my dream job.

But I was pushing myself too hard. My parents noticed it first. On our video calls, they'd say how my face looked as if I'd lost weight. Then they asked why my energy seemed lower. I tried to shrug it off. My parents are an ocean away from me; it was possible they didn't quite see the real me on the video calls. But a couple weeks after their comments on my unhealthy appearance, I began feeling pains in my stomach. I was also cold, shivering. And although I was hungry, I had no appetite. I wasn't sick. The stress of the job hunt was impacting my body.

Looking back, the warning signs had happened long before that day; I was just so focused on the hunt that I didn't notice. Finally, my body yelled at me, "Hey, Mike! Wake up!" The pain and awful feeling lasted for a few days.

On the next call with my parents, I admitted to my dad that he might have been right. "I think you're on to something," I told him. "Maybe I need to take a break."

COVID restrictions were starting to be lifted at that time, and my parents were planning on taking a trip to the U.S. to see my sisters, grandkids, and me. So my parents and I planned a getaway trip to Alaska for a week. That's when I fully comprehended how much I needed a break. Being in nature, with no cell service, having quality time with my family … I needed it all.

When I returned home, I felt refreshed. I slowly picked up the job hunt again and … four months later I accepted a position with Yelp. The perfect position for me!

The point of my story: Realize that the people in your inner circle care about you. They don't want to see you burnt out, exhausted, sick, and weak because of the stress of your job hunt (or for any reason, really). They will mention something to you, eventually. But at the end of the day, it really is up to you to accept their feedback and measure it against what your body is telling you.

It is important to measure that honestly. If someone says you're losing weight, that your voice is different, or you're off in some way, you have to stop and ask if there's any truth in that. Nobody will ever know you as well as you know yourself and your body, which might be ironic considering how easy it is for us not to listen to our bodies!

Your friends and family might see symptoms, but you will be the only one to know what's going on. You have to listen to your body. It will tell you how you're doing. It might start off soft and subtle, but if you ignore it, it will get louder and harder. Listen to it. Check in with yourself. And, whether someone in your inner circle notices or not, take a break when your body tells you that you're not as grounded as you think you are.

Celebrate Your Wins

As I kept seeing people getting offers and moving on with their careers, it only became harder and harder to stay motivated to continue. I remember getting lost in the kinds of thoughts that sent me down negative emotional rabbit holes. *Am I good enough? What's going on? Why is everyone moving on but me?*

I was fortunate to have my sister in my corner. She may not have been able to give me a solution on how to handle a particular interview, but she was there for me to lean against when the journey was particularly painful. Additionally, her pep talks helped me realize I was further along in the process than I'd realized, which helped breathe new life into my job-hunting sails.

If you don't have sisters like mine, let her advice remind you: When you're feeling down, take stock of where you are, inventory everything you've learned, and celebrate all the new skills you have gained.

It took me over a year to find a new job when I wanted to move from Mattel. A year of me learning from all the research I did to close the gap and learning from all the practicing for interviews. I started bringing the learning into my day job, without quite thinking about it. And those learnings were paying dividends that I didn't quite realize at the time—not until my sister pointed them out. But, once I realized what was happening, it became fuel for me to continue. That proof showing me how far I'd come was a great motivator to continue believing in myself and to keep going.

I began seeing things a little bit differently. I started modifying the way I coach my direct reports, and I approached problem-solving in new ways.

In short, I became better at my job, something that didn't go unnoticed. When I finally left Mattel, one of the senior executives told me he felt that I had really stepped up and brought a breath of fresh air to the project I had been working on. His exact words were, "It sucks, because I thought we were just about to redo a lot of great things with you, but now Yelp will get to have that experience."

His words were so validating to me! They confirmed what I'd been telling myself all along: Every failed job interview was a good thing. It helped me get better.

I suggest you start getting in the habit of similar reframing.

You can look at an interview follow-up in which you receive a "no, thank you" as a failure that depresses you. Or, you can look at it for what it is: an opportunity to grow. If you want to be a better professional, or even a better person, you have to welcome failure as a painful learning opportunity. Similarly to how your body experiences pain after a hard workout as it gets stronger, you have to experience some pain in your job hunt for your skills to improve and to build the psychological resilience to support yourself.

To go a step further, don't just see your failures as learning opportunities. Try to look at every discovery that you're doing better as something worth celebrating. Celebrate it!

To be clear: I'm not suggesting you celebrate everything for the sake of celebrating. I'm talking about celebrating your wins. It's taking a page out of the professional athlete playbook. And it's something I wish I had discovered much earlier on my career track!

Take the time to periodically stop and evaluate how far you've come. That is especially important to do when you're feeling down. Compare what you knew at the beginning of your job hunt with what you know now, and acknowledge how much you've grown. Whether that is something you've learned, something you are now doing in a better way, or something that is getting you better results, it is something to celebrate. With it, you'll be able to tap into the energy of motivation and keep going.

Pat yourself on the back each time you get that "aha" feeling of understanding something new or when you feel you rocked an answer by connecting dots—even in mock interviews.

Celebrate breakthroughs, even the breakthroughs that come from interviews that didn't go well, because you will learn something or get something out of them that you can apply in another interview or elsewhere in your life. As with most new things—opportunities, adventures, life cycles, etc.—conflict and struggle often come first; breakthroughs will only occur as you grind your way through. We should be celebrating the breakthroughs because that means you're learning something. Learning is always worth celebrating.

At a recent seminar, I heard world champion triathlete and Olympic coach Siri Lindley speak. One of the things she encouraged everyone to do was celebrate their wins. In her mind, there is no failing; if nothing else, you're learning from your experiences. When you capture them in a moment of celebration, you reinforce that learning. Give yourself the grace to pat yourself on the back!

The Right Time and the Right Reasons

By learning to support myself by having a job-hunting partner, taking advantage of the resources available to me, and listening to my family and body, I was able to support myself through the long journey of switching industries in my career. That mental and emotional capacity, coupled with all the research I'd been doing, got me into the later rounds of interviews. In fact, it got to the point where I just knew I'd make it past the first and even second rounds because I knew my answers were very strong. But I still got rejected by several.

Rejections always sting, but they sting a lot less when you can remind yourself that they are not personal.

The truth is, there are so many different factors, most of which are beyond what you can control, that influence whether you get a call back after an interview. You might be interviewed by someone who is having a bad day, or who just heard some bad news and they're having trouble truly focusing on you. It's possible that you're just not a good fit at the moment. It's possible that you *are* a good fit for the job, except they really need someone they don't have to train on a particular software that another candidate knows.

So it helps to remember that sometimes being rejected is simply outside of your control, regardless of how it feels.

The hiring managers have their own goals and perspectives when it comes to interviews. So let's look at what it's like to be a hiring manager. By being able to see things as they do, you'll be more resilient when it comes to rejection—and you'll be even better prepared for your interviews.

CHAPTER 4

IT'S ABOUT RISK

I made it pretty far in the interviewing process at SpaceX. I was so far in that when the company narrowed the candidates down to just two people, I was one of them. But then they chose the other candidate.

When the recruiter called to tell me of their decision, I thanked them for considering me, and I asked for feedback on how I could have performed better. I also asked why they chose the other person and not me. I didn't whine about it; I was genuinely curious and hoped to learn how I could become an even better candidate the next time I applied somewhere.

The recruiter had already collected feedback from the whole hiring team, so her answer wasn't biased from her perspective only. What she told me was that it was consistent across the board: The team thought I was talented. They had no doubt that if they hired me, I would be highly successful at my job within three months. So, really, I was a great potential prospect for the position.

The other candidate, though, had an edge over me. Remember, at that time I was hoping to make a switch into the tech industry. The other candidate was already there; they came from the tech industry, so there would be less required to get them up to speed with the job. They wouldn't need three months to be successful; SpaceX could plug and play them right away.

I appreciated hearing that feedback. It was good to know they saw me in the light I wanted to be seen in. And it gave me a glimpse of what all goes into hiring decisions. By understanding why they went with another candidate, I was able to see from the hiring manager's perspective.

Everyone is busy with their day-to-day job. When a hiring manager brings a new person to the team, they add to the team's already full plate of responsibilities. Now, they have to help the new hire fill in the knowledge and experience gaps before the new hire can be fully functional. Therefore, the less they have to train that person on, the more time and energy they'll have for juggling all their other responsibilities. Plus, there's less risk of the new hire failing and wasting all their time.

Because I've found myself in the hiring manager's position, I have an even fuller understanding of what it's like to sit in that seat. Back when I was trying to make a career switch, I had no idea what the whole process was like for the hiring manager, nor did I fully comprehend the risks they take with each new hire. If I had, I may have been a little more compassionate toward many of them, and I may have gone easier on myself, knowing that I was often a risky new hire.

The Process

A hiring manager's job isn't easy. It's actually a lot of work and stress to hire someone. Before we can even open up a role, we have to fight for it, meaning we must make a proposal to leadership that justifies why we need an additional head to count. Each position is a cost to the company, after all, so we have to present a case as to how, by filling this position, we'll be able to make more money or achieve a goal that makes the position worth funding.

We even have to do this when we are replacing an employee. Frequently, when someone leaves a company, there will be an attempt to make the team more efficient instead of just replacing them. With each position that opens, the executive team may want to analyze whether it makes sense to put a person back in that spot or if moving the funds for it to a different position would make more of an impact. They may even reevaluate whether it's necessary to have anyone new come on board at all.

Getting approval is just one hurdle. After it comes in, you must write the job description. Every company does things a little differently, but for most hiring managers, you must spend time writing or revising a job description. You then coordinate with HR to identify how the interviews will happen within the confines of the company's structure. The resumes come streaming in at that point, which means it's time for you to review and vet candidates.

By the way, while all that is happening, you're still doing your regular job. So when you identify what seems to be a great selection of candidates, it then becomes time to play Tetris with your calendar every day to fit in the candidates based on their availability and your other responsibilities. Additionally, like many other hiring managers, I always spend time going through each person's application and thinking through the questions I want to ask. I prepare for each interview individually based on the differences I see in their resumes—which has a huge impact on my time.

After each interview, hiring managers must thoroughly document every single one of them. You must put on paper—or in an electronic document— your evaluation of each candidate. Often, you then have a panel discussion with the people on the hiring team to compare notes. The hiring manager has the final say, but we do take into consideration what each member of the hiring panel thinks about each candidate.

It's a long process, and that all happens before an offer is made!

After the offer comes the negotiation. While the hiring manager may not be the person who does the actual negotiating with the candidate, they are the one who must go to the benefits team and fight for the candidate to see what they can get for them. Whether it's for a candidate who cannot start on the day they're expected to, a candidate who wants additional pay, or something else, we have to present a case to HR and leadership, hoping we can get them and the candidate to agree on terms.

If the negotiations fail, and the first-choice candidate declines the offer, we have to reach out to the second-choice candidate and start negotiations all over again—or even start the interview process from scratch.

Long story short: It's a taxing process to hire someone, and each candidate has a risk factor—not everyone will work out. So we do what we can to mitigate that risk, which is often why we take the plug-and-play route.

Why Plug-and-Play Is the Safest Way

Do know that hiring managers or recruiters are not intentionally trying to be jerks. When they ask difficult questions or challenge your projects, that's because they are trying to root out what you know, what other skills you have, or whether you will be a good fit with the company. Their job is to do what is in the best interest of the company, after all.

They need to ask the difficult questions to determine whether you can do the job because if they hire you and you can't, then it's more time, money, and energy for the company to get you up to speed—or even to find another candidate.

So they do tend to be cautious, and they may ask harder and harder questions the further you go in the process.

I know I'm often more specific, some might say more critical, on some of the questions I ask when I realize the candidate before me is switching careers or functions. When I do, it's not because I'm trying to dash anyone's dreams. It's because someone lacking experience or background for a career switch puts me at a higher risk of having to start the whole process all over again should that person not work out.

For the most part, we hiring managers will often lean toward the person who has the most experience for the position. We like to hire people we can plug and play right away, versus spending six months to train them and hope they can master the job.

For example, let's say someone at Netflix was in the process of screening candidates for a software engineer position. If they see someone who was a software engineer for someplace like Google for years, most likely their job is similar enough that they can be plugged into the team at Netflix with a short learning curve. That potential makes them a better candidate than someone who's in a hardware engineering job employed by a small private finance company.

Additionally, there's a second component to why plug and play is sometimes the way a hiring manager will base their decisions. Some companies like to rotate their managers to different teams in order to make that manager more well-rounded. This actually happened to me at Mattel. The company believes you should touch the different types of businesses they have so that you can be a better leader. That's great, because you really do learn a lot. However, I was there for five years, during which time I was on five different teams—meaning every year I was learning a new type of business.

So when I was hiring people to work on my teams, I gravitated toward the plug-and-play candidates. It would often take three months to find the right candidates and another three for the interviewing process. If it would then take me three more months to get a new employee fully up to speed, that would only leave three months with my team at full capacity before I'd be rotated to a different business.

Like everyone else, I had business goals I was trying to reach, so the right person would usually be an experienced candidate. That person would carry a lower risk. Additionally, the less time I was required to spend training the person, the more time I'd be able to spend on helping the company reach its goals.

It may not seem fair, but you have to look at it from the company's perspective. When a job position is open, it's because the company has a need that is going unmet. And that need remains unmet as long as that position is vacant *plus* the amount of time it takes to get the new person up to speed. It only makes sense that they would prefer to have that role filled by someone who would need less time.

A plug-and-play candidate also takes fewer resources, as it can be very expensive to train someone: It takes quite a bit of energy, time, and attention from other people who probably have full plates as it is. And, it's risky: What if the new hire proves unable to do the job in the end?

When the Risk Doesn't Pay Off

I was once assigned to manage a team of interns. Most of them were really excited for the opportunity—most. One of them, whom I'll call David, didn't seem passionate about the job at all. It felt like he didn't even care whether he had the job—he was just going through the motions to put in his time.

At that company, each intern was required to work on a specific project, at the end of which I'd make sure they had the opportunity to present it to the executive board. If they did well on their presentation and impressed the executives, it would greatly increase their chance of getting an offer to return to the company.

I arranged for the chief design officer of the company and a couple of VPs to get on board with reviewing the projects, which meant my reputation was also on the line. After all, I had just wrangled someone pretty high up in the company to come sit down for 60 minutes to watch an intern presentation—the last thing I wanted to do was make them feel as if they had wasted their time.

When it was time for David to prepare for his presentation, it seemed like I cared more about whether he did well than he did. I spent an overload of hours guiding him on his project. Then, I tried to foster his growth by helping him prepare to present it. Once again, I spent more hours of my time and more taxing of my energy reserves doing something that wasn't my primary responsibility. All because I didn't want to risk him failing.

I wound up warning my manager that the presentation might not go well—and I was right. It didn't. It put me in a bad spot. It was concerning because at the end of the day, the chief design officer and other executives could have questioned my ability to manage and lead. Fortunately, my manager assured me it would not tarnish my reputation with the company, and that he'd speak with the chief design officer and other executives in the room about it.

When the risk doesn't pay off with an intern, you know you just lost three months. But when it's a full-time employee you're committed to bringing up to speed, how long do you wait before you acknowledge that they're not the right person? Ninety days? Six months?

Which is the best way to look at it? Realize early on that the person isn't the right fit and let them go, or keep them on beyond when it's productive to do so to help nurture them? Choosing the former means the company's resources spent training is minimized and the candidate's time finding a better-fitting job is maximized. But what does that say about a hiring manager if they bring on people who are the wrong fit?

In comparison, some say they choose the latter option out of care for the candidate, and that due to the time already invested by both parties, they owe it to them to offer the extra guidance or, alternatively, see if they would be more successful elsewhere in the company. But how do you determine what's in their best interest?

Having a new hire not work out can be quite a complex situation, to say the least. But hopefully it's clear that hiring anyone is a risk.

So when you're turned down for a job, know it's never anything personal. There are numerous factors that come into play and many considerations that go into the decision of whether to hire someone.

There Is Still Hope

At this point, you may be thinking it's hopeless. Why should you bother trying to make a career switch when it sounds almost impossible to do? Well, you should do it if it's something you really want to do, and you should know there is still hope.

There are numerous factors that can come into play when hiring managers look at you. As we've just covered, this can work against you, true, but it can also work *for* you instead. In fact, I frequently hire career switchers—always have. And that includes at Mattel, where I rotated through businesses. While there, I hired people from the music industry, sports teams, and even the entertainment industry to work with me at a toy company.

The main reason why I did so is because they exhibited pure talent. How they conducted themselves during interviews, answered questions, or proved their logical thinking and problem-solving skills when I presented a test-case scenario all came through during the interview process.

The second reason I'd hire a career switcher is that they were often much more passionate about the job. There's a famous quote from Herb Kelleher: "You don't hire for skills, you hire for attitude. You can always teach skills."

For me, I can definitely say that when someone has the enthusiasm to learn and a passion for the subject, I often value that over someone who has the technical skills required for the job but comes off as unmotivated or blasé during an interview.

Of course, it still depends on the position, how much the person would have to learn, and if the job definitely requires a specific set of skills or technical expertise. Those factors could make me lean toward a non-career-switcher.

A third reason I'd hire a career switcher is because they are someone who would make for an excellent fit for the team. If I have a lot of right-brain types on my team, then I may lean toward finding a candidate who is more left-brain to add a little balance. If I have several extroverts, maybe we need more introverts. Or if we have a lot of macro strategic thinkers, I may look for someone who will be more detail-oriented. It might be because they will fit with the overall energy of the team or help create a more diverse or well-rounded team. Any of those factors may help you on your journey.

The experience and expertise you can bring from your function in a different industry might be seen as a bonus to a hiring manager. When I started my current role at Yelp, it was my first tech company position, but my consumer-product and retail industry experience enabled me to bring a different approach to solving problems. In the feedback I've received, it's been mentioned that I brought in a fresh way of looking at things. So coming from a different industry or job function can benefit a hiring team.

I promise, this journey is not a definite dead end. Just expect it to take some time and know that there are factors outside of your control that are working against you. However, if you want the change badly enough, and you work hard to minimize your gaps, you can increase your odds and present your different work experience as a feature, not a bug. You don't have to be the standard candidate if you stand out positively enough to be the exception.

There Are Exceptions

If you're not an exact match for the job, the risk of hiring you can be mitigated if someone the hiring manager knows vouches for you. If that third party says you're really good—that you have drive, a good work ethic, or are a great problem solver—that will encourage the hiring manager to look a little closer at you.

I was on a hiring team with several other people when someone I knew applied for a job. He bombed his official interview with me, but I had a conversation with the hiring manager.

"Look, based on this interview, I would not move him forward," I said. "But, I know the quality of his work. He's excellent."

My words must have held some weight, because he was called back for another interview, then subsequently made it to the final round.

By having a connection to the company, you take away some of the fears a hiring manager may have. They don't really know anything about you except for what your resume shows. So they don't know your true capability. Again, you are a risk for them. However, if someone they know can recommend you, that fear and risk are mitigated.

You Must Be Committed

Regardless of how well connected you are or how well you've bridged the gap to make yourself a good candidate, for a hiring manager to feel confident in offering you a job, they must know you are committed to working it.

Almost contradictorily, it's common advice when looking for a job to think about the next one you'll want so that you can pave the way for your future. But that doesn't mean you should look for a job to have for six months while you're looking for a better one. If a hiring manager gets the feeling you have no intention of staying long in a position, that could be a mark against you.

Generally, I can tell from most of the people I interview whether they are committed to the job, and it's something I try to home in on. Think about it: Would you want to hire someone if you know they'll quit in six months?

Sometimes, the answer to that question might actually be *yes*, because the person is so very talented that it might be worth it. But if they will take six months to train ... that's a different story.

You may think this goes against what we discussed in Chapter 1—about potentially seeing yourself in a job as a stepping stone to the ideal career you're aiming toward. It's not. The difference is commitment. If the person I'm interviewing is committed to the job I need to fill, even though they have a bigger vision for their career, I'll still consider them a potential good hire because commitment matters.

I am the first to admit that when I accepted the position at Mattel, I knew it was a stepping stone to what I thought, at the time, was my ultimate job: marketing for an entertainment company. But I was able to commit to Mattel because it fit into my overall why of my career switch and resonated with what I valued about the entertainment industry.

A good friend of mine was an animator at Pixar. She's usually a very reserved, introverted person, but when she speaks about her job, she lights up. She used to volunteer at a hospital and had witnessed children with cancer or other illnesses find relief by watching animated movies. She told me, "When the children watched the cartoons, they forgot about their pain and suffering." I love that concept! It reminded me of my aunt. She was a dentist who put monitors on the chairs so that children could watch cartoons while getting their teeth tended to; that entertainment helped keep their fear of the dentist at bay.

That power, that ability of a movie or some kind of entertainment to distract people from pain, possibly even providing them with some relief, is one of the things that fueled my desire to switch to that industry. It is in alignment with my why: When I was younger, cartoons were always my favorite escape after a bad day at school. Whenever a teacher was hard on me or I was bullied by a classmate because I didn't speak English well, I'd come home and turn on the TV. My worries would disappear for at least 30 minutes while Scooby-Doo distracted me with his shenanigans.

When I realized I could go for a marketing position at Mattel, I thought it could be a good stepping stone to further my career. It would give me a great opportunity to go into marketing and grow as a marketer. And, because so many toys are based on movies, there was an entertainment connection to it. So I didn't see Mattel as just a job I'd have for six months while I looked for my next one. I saw it as a role that I could give 105% of my energy to while learning and expanding professionally as much as possible. I was excited about the role.

While I may not have been planning to spend the rest of my life working at Mattel, I was all in to do the best I could for at least the next couple of years. And I knew that when the time would come for me to make my next move—which at that time I expected to be to an entertainment company—I'd be in a much better place professionally. Because I was committed to my position at Mattel, I was present enough to succeed and let the job itself open a new future for me.

Embrace the Uphill Battle

If you've made it this far in the book and you're thinking, "Making a career switch is like an uphill battle," know that you're right. So you need to be prepared for it.

If nothing else, I hope what you took from this section is that you must be committed to making the switch and that you must be committed to putting in your all once you're in the job. You can't just think about it like putting a check in a box until you make it to your "real" goal; you also must be flexible, allowing your life to unfold so you can see what it presents to you.

I don't know what life would be like for me today if I was working in a film studio, but I can tell you I'm very happy with my life now and how it's progressed—none of that would have been possible if I was just in my jobs to get a paycheck.

Still, it is a lot of work and potential stress to make a career switch. That's why it's imperative that you're certain the timing is right and that your desire to make a switch is something that is a true want or need. My firsthand experience is proof that if you want something badly enough, and you know *why* you want it badly enough, when the going gets tough, you won't quit.

Honestly, though, I can say the ultimate reason I was successful is because I was doing it at the right time and for the right reasons—in other words, I had a strong enough motivation.

One of the most important things to understand regarding a career switch is that if you don't truly feel motivated to make a change, then it will be hard to maintain your enthusiasm and drive to continue the hunt when things get rough. If you ever find yourself questioning whether or not making the switch is the right path, wondering if it's worth all the effort and hard work involved, then perhaps this isn't the right time for you to be making the switch.

Motivation to keep on going is found when you're able to tap into your why. Why do you want to make the change? It's okay if you don't know the exact answer right now. The next part of the book will help you find your why, or reinforce it so it can support you and give you the motivation necessary to keep on keeping on when the going gets tough.

PART 2

PRACTICAL TIPS AND FRAMEWORKS TO MAKE THE CHANGE LESS DIFFICULT

CHAPTER 5

THE REAL WHY IS THE ONLY ONE THAT MATTERS

O ne of my favorite quotes is from Jack Ma: "Today is difficult. Tomorrow is more difficult. And the day after tomorrow is beautiful. Most people die tomorrow evening."[3] Ma was actually talking about his approach to business. What he means is that most people give up before they reach their goals.

I stumbled upon the video of him saying that around the time I decided to accept my job with Yelp. His words resonated with me because that's how the path of my career switch felt. I had a long today and an even longer tomorrow, but, at the moment, I was about to start my day after tomorrow.

By now, you know how difficult you can expect a career switch to be. In order for you to ride out the difficult todays and even more difficult tomorrows, you need a strong anchor to keep you motivated. You need to have conviction and know why you're doing this in order to stand firm throughout the storm. And, in my opinion, the best way to develop that strong, anchoring sense of conviction is to be certain about why you're making this transition in the first place.

Your "why," knowing what it is and tapping into it frequently, will be what prevents you from quitting before the beautiful day after tomorrow.

---

3   Jack Ma, "APEC CEO SUMMIT 2015: Insights from Alibaba's Jack Ma," posted November 17, 2015, by Rappler, YouTube, https://youtu.be/BbfYcEnjFk0?si=TZpsM92rPvrLXi_L&t=990.

Determination in Adversity

As you may recall, when I accepted a marketing position with Mattel, it was really only a function-only switch (I know, "only"!). Regardless, my ultimate goal was a marketing position in a tech or entertainment company.

Mattel gave me the opportunity to prove myself in marketing. It also exposed me to the tech sector when the company wanted to try bridging technology with toys. I truly enjoyed my job—I loved the marketing aspect, and I appreciated the learning opportunity it provided.

However, people around me were changing careers. Every time I'd get together with friends, I'd discover yet another one of them had made a career switch. My class reunion was full of people excited about moving into a new gig in a new role or a new industry. Even my manager at Mattel had moved to a new position in the tech industry. Call it FOMO: I wanted a piece of that excitement. I thought it would be cool to make a career switch, too, and keep up with my peers.

So I started looking and applying. Rejections piled up. My enthusiasm and motivation dialed down. I started questioning why I was putting myself through such torment, and I realized I'd fallen into the trap of peer pressure: Everyone else was doing it, so perhaps I should, too. That didn't make the rejections worthwhile, so I quit looking for a while. To return to Jack Ma's quote again, I died the evening before the day after tomorrow.

So, I paused and took a minute to think about things and reevaluate. Really, I gave up on the job hunt. I focused on my role at Mattel and really enjoyed it. However, a year or so later, my life evolved. Changes happened that got me thinking about changing careers again.

I looked at where I was compared to where I wanted to be, both personally and professionally. Personally, I wanted a new home in a different part of town, which happened to be more expensive. Extra income would be required to pay for that.

Professionally, my experience working on the tech toy created a curiosity within me to learn more about the tech industry. My experience at Mattel had shown that people in the tech world problem-solve differently from people in the consumer product or toy industry. I wanted to develop those new intellectual muscles because ultimately, I wanted to be an executive one day—a well-rounded one, which meant having different muscles to flex.

So, I ruminated and went deep into the whys behind both my personal and professional desires. That introspection allowed me to understand that I wanted the peace of mind of knowing that my basic needs of survival and stability were met financially, which would free me up to chase after things I *wanted* to do without worrying about covering what I *had* to do.

Equally, the call to learn more, to depart the safety of doing what I was doing and learn something new in a new position, fueled a realization. The more I explored why I wanted a career change, the more I realized it was about legacy. I enjoy influencing people, and I believe my legacy will be through the people I mentor and coach.

When I looked at where I wanted to be in my life in 10 years, or even 20, I saw myself as an executive, someone in a position with a broader reach to be a positive influence on others. At the end of the day, I understood that if I wanted to achieve that level to leave a legacy—my immortality, as some athletes call it—then I'd better learn as many different ways of thinking as possible.

Because I had reached such a deep level of clarity about my why, I was able to tap into the emotional aspect of it when things got tough. In that way, I kept up my motivation to continue my job search. Even when my parents were telling me I needed to take a break, my why continued to fuel me.

If I had been telling myself I was making a career switch just because I wanted more money, I don't think I would have been able to follow through on it. I'm not sure if the difficulty of the journey would have been worth an increase in pay alone, regardless of how determined I felt at the outset.

Without clearly understanding the why, determination by itself can only go so far. Imagine being stranded on a remote island, exhausted and battered, with no sign of rescue. Or picture yourself lost in a freezing wilderness, without clothes or shelter, as night closes in. Will you still be as determined? In other words, determination is important. It's what fuels your desire to get somewhere. But, in addition to determination, you need to understand your why. Knowing what your why is, and reminding yourself of it, will help you stay determined in the face of whatever adversity may be blocking your way.

I think many people believe that being determined is what it takes to get wherever they want to go in life. While determination is good, there is so much more to what's required to make a career switch—determination is like the tip of the iceberg that shows above the water line. What's underneath, what's supporting the determination is hard work, learning, resilience, and—perhaps what's most important because it's what fuels all the rest—something that's internally motivating you. Your why.

Remembering Your Why

Perhaps it's ironic, but sometimes it's hard to remember your why. Yes, you can get so busy or distracted through the twists and turns of your career switch that you lose sight of why you're doing it. So, before we move on to talk about how to discover your why, I'd like to share a tool I used to help me maintain my focus on it and never lose sight of it.

This might seem backward. After all, shouldn't you know your why first, and then figure out how to remember it? But once you hear about the tool, you'll understand.

I made what's often referred to as a vision board. I collected images that represented how I wanted my life to look like, images that resonated with my why, and made a collage of sorts that I turned into the desktop image on my computer. That way, I saw it every day. Other people will create a vision board on an actual posterboard that they hang somewhere easily visible. You can even put it on your phone. The idea is to create one and put it someplace where you'll see it every day.

Similar to visualizing where you want to go in life, your vision board will reinforce your why each time you look at it and remind you why you are doing whatever it is that you are doing.

Other ideas include placing Post-it notes or handwritten inspiring words in predominant spots in your environment. This approach may work better for those of you who are word people, not image people.

Whatever you do, put your vision board where you cannot ignore it. As I said, mine's on my computer because I sit down in front of it every day. I've heard of a man who taped his on the ceiling directly above his bed so that it was the first thing he saw when he woke up each morning.

So, as you work through the process of discovering your why, think about how you can visualize or summarize each aspect to create your own vision board or notes to remind you of where you want to be.

CHAPTER 6

HOW TO FIND YOUR WHY

Jim Rohn, a motivational speaker and mentor of Tony Robbins, used to frequently remind people that "reasons come first, answers come second."[4] Your why is your reason, which means you figure that out first; then, the answers for how to achieve your reasons will come next. In other words, once you have a clear conviction about why you want to make a career switch, you can begin the process of figuring out how to make that happen.

There are numerous ways to discover your why. My favorite is the Seven Whys, which I learned about in business school. In full transparency, I'm sharing with you a screenshot of my own results when I went through this process. As I mentioned, I wanted to make a career change from my marketing position at Mattel to a marketing position in a tech company for two reasons: because I wanted to develop more intellectual muscles, and because I wanted to increase my salary.

This first one is about my personal development. I started with the following questions:

Question	Reason
Why do you want to work as the [job title] for [company] at [location]?	Reason #1: I want to work as the [job title] for [company] at [location] because ... [reason #1]

---

4 Tony Robbins, Unleash the Power Within, live event, March 21-24, 2024.

Why [reason #1]?	Reason #2
Why [reason #2]?	Reason #3
Why [reason #3]?	Reason #4
Why [reason #4]?	Reason #5
Why [reason #5]?	Reason #6
Why [reason #6]?	Reason #7

First, I entered my dream job (product marketing manager), company (Amazon), and location (Los Angeles). Then, I asked why I wanted it. The key thing to think about as you go through this exercise is to poke holes in each of your answers to force yourself to get deeper and deeper into your true motivations. Here's what I did:

1. Why did I want to work in product marketing in the tech industry? My initial reason for wanting that job was to develop or learn innovative thinking techniques.
    a. Poking holes: Clearly, a career switch was not the only avenue I had for doing that. I could have taken courses, gone to seminars, read books, etc. So there was more to it, which means asking:
2. Why do I want to develop new muscles and innovative thinking? At the time, I felt I was too one-dimensional, which was holding me back from achieving my career goal of becoming an executive leader.
    a. Again, there were other options I could have chosen that would have developed executive-leader-type muscles: I could have worked with a career coach or I could have found a mentor. So ...
3. Why did I want to be an executive? As I thought about it, I realized I truly enjoyed leading and mentoring others through real-life projects.
    a. Frankly, I could do that in the role that I already had at Mattel, where I frequently worked with interns and specialists.

Which meant there was more to my desire for a career switch. I needed to keep asking why.

4. Why do I want to be a leader or mentor? Because it gives me fulfillment.

    a. Things got interesting with this answer! I realized I wanted to have more of a positive impact, to have more influence on others. One of the best ways to do that is to move up the corporate ladder, to be dynamic, and to have multifaceted experience. When I was working on the tech toy project, I could see there was a gap between where I was and where I needed to be in order to create the kind of impact I wanted to create. But was there more?

5. Why does creating a positive impact matter to me? I realized that it meant my work has a sense of purpose.

    a. I'd never really thought this deeply before about my career. Going through this exercise really helped me home in on a sense of destiny and a desire for my life to have meaning that I never knew I had before. It was exciting, even as I dug deeper. I knew the higher I could go in the corporate world, the more influence I could have. But to be a good, dynamic leader, I needed a broader set of experiences: I needed to grow new muscles.

6. Why do I want my work to have purpose? Because it's how I create a professional legacy—it's how I leave something behind.

    a. Pretty powerful, right? Could there be more?

7. Why is leaving something behind important to me? Because that's how I achieve immortality.

Looking over my answers, you can see that by number five, I had enough to fire up some passion for making my job switch. And that is often the case. However, I suggest always trying to get to seven levels of why, because you just might uncover something that you haven't thought about. You're really forced to think hard when it comes to those last two answers; they don't come naturally.

No Right Answers

It's important that you don't get caught up on providing what you think is the "right" answer. All your answers must come from within you, and they may only apply to you. Which is fine—this exercise is all about you: who you are and who you want to be. Your responses don't have to apply to anyone else or even make sense to anyone else. So, don't aim for perfect sequencing or to have all your dots neatly lined up. Aim for getting to the deepest why that resonates within you, and that will be strong enough to anchor you as you go through your career switch. As long as you arrive at something that gives you conviction, that's all that matters.

Let's look at my second reason for making a career switch: more money.

1. Why do I want this job? To make more money.
    a. There are other options for this. For example, I could get a part-time gig.
2. Why do I want more money? I want to be able to afford a monthly mortgage.
    a. I could have stayed living where I was or even downsized, so, again, a career switch wasn't the only answer here.
3. Why do I want to afford a monthly mortgage? To provide a stable environment for myself and, hopefully, my future family.
    a. I had a stable environment. Really, I wanted a nicer one in a different community, one that would be better suited for my maturing self and a future family. So, why was that important?
4. Why do I want a stable environment? I see it as my responsibility to secure my basic needs, so I don't have to rely on others and so I don't have to worry about making sure my needs are met.
    a. That was an interesting and somewhat surprising answer to me.

5. Why do you want to fulfill that responsibility? I wanted the peace of mind that I would always be secure and that my future family would be taken care of.

   a. Peace of mind and security are pretty strong whys. But I continued to dig deeper.

6. Why do you want peace of mind and security? A few answers came up for me here. One was: because that would mean I'd have more freedom. By not worrying about covering my basic needs, I'd have more freedom to do other things I wanted to do (like writing a book). The second answer really hit me hard: I understood that by securing my basic needs, I was ensuring my survival.

   a. Freedom and survival are core human drivers. Tapping into that sent my motivation into a higher gear. It sounds dramatic, I know, but realizing my career switch would impact my ability to live free and survive was like adding fuel to my motivation.

7. Why do I want to secure my survival? Because it gives me the control to live and experience life under my own terms.

To go back to the vision board idea I suggested in the previous chapter, when I would look (daily!) at what I created on my vision board, I would remember my whys—immortality, freedom, and owning my life narrative. Rarely did I think, *Oh, and I'll make more money, too*, or, *I'll be more well-rounded*. Always, though, I'd feel a surge of energy to want to continue with my career switch. That's how I knew my why was strong enough, that I had the conviction to follow through on the journey to a new position.

Try It on for Size

Now it's your turn to go through this exercise. With each answer, you'll see there's a goal that pops up. Take that goal and ask why you want it in the next question. Do this seven times. Keep in mind that this is an emotional exercise, so don't try to aim for perfect, rational thoughts. And remember, no one will ever see these answers but you—unless you choose to share them, which you don't have to do. So be honest with your answers. Always remember that none of them are wrong and that this is just a tool to help you get clarity.

I also encourage you to do this framework more than once. In fact, go through it in one sitting. Set it aside and ignore it for a couple of days. Then do it again. Ideally, do it three times within the span of a week. Then compare your answers, watching for consistency. If you come up with drastically different answers, then there's probably something you need to iron out within yourself first. You may be too scattered to properly focus on your career-switching activities at this time. And that's okay.

It's also okay to have multiple whys. As you can see in my example, leaving a legacy and ensuring my survival are two very different things. But they are compatible things, and that's what matters. If you come up with widely different answers that are so far apart they cannot be connected, then maybe take a step back and spend more time getting clarity on your life and career goals.

In the same vein, don't reject any answers outright—they all represent parts of you where you are at this time in your life. The important thing is to get as much clarity as possible into your authentic self. And if you have consistency among your answers then you'll really understand what you want, and you won't waver when things get tough. You won't question your why.

When Siri Lindly spoke about becoming a triathlete, she mentioned that she barely knew how to swim. So when she went to train with her coach, it was hard work. She easily could have quit after the first week—possibly even after the first day—because her body's aches and pains made her all too aware of how steep her uphill journey would be. But she didn't. Instead, she went on to become a world triathlete champion.

What kept her going? She had conviction. She knew her why. As she explained later in an interview, "I was at a stage in my life where I was so desperate to find out who I was and what I was made of. And triathlon presented itself as a perfect vehicle through which I could find myself, test my limits, and earn my own respect for myself."[5]

What's your why? What will keep you going day after day after day when it would be much easier to just quit?

Once you've delved into each of the layers that make up your why, and generated the motivation you'll need to follow through, it's time to learn the framework that will help you focus on landing the job of your (current) dreams.

---

5   Mark Athitakis, "Four Keys to Motivation From a World-Champion Triathlete," Associations Now, July 15, 2018, https://associationsnow.com/2018/07/four-keys-to-motivation-from-a-world-champion-triathlete/.

CHAPTER 7

THE ONE-PAGER

Fueled by knowing for sure what I wanted to do and why, I applied for another product marketer position (similar to what I was doing at Mattel), this time with Amazon. Again, the position meant I would have better opportunities for expanding my thinking and skill set. I still found that prospect very exciting. I was also eager to work in tech. It's hard to be more tech-oriented than Amazon! Oh, and the pay was very attractive.

Now that you've gone through the exercise to get to the root of *your* why, you understand why I always encourage people to not let "more money" be the only reason for finding a new job. However, we cannot ignore the impact money has on our lives. Out of total transparency, one of the reasons I later found the position at Yelp so attractive was the income potential it promised. I lived in Los Angeles and wanted to buy a place that was closer to the beach and in a safe neighborhood. Such a home would require a pretty large down payment and substantial mortgage payments. So, if I were to say money wasn't an issue as I looked for a job, I would be lying to some extent. It was definitely part of what incentivized me.

But, to get back to the Amazon position … I had a vision of what it would be like to be a product marketing manager there, and I got really close to getting that job. Perhaps if I had completed the framework below, I would have. However, what got me close was all the other prep work I did beforehand.

Getting Ready to Get Ready

The price of housing where I wanted to live was more than I could easily afford. That assured me I'd need to go into an industry that paid a little more than the traditional retail or consumer products industry. Thankfully, my newfound admiration and interest in the tech space would fit the bill here.

Knowing the industry narrowed the field of potential companies where I should look for work. But I needed to consider several other factors before I could target specific ones.

One thing that influenced my decision was thinking about the job I thought I'd want to go for after this one. As I've mentioned before, there may be several jobs for you to use as stepping stones before you can land your dream job. If you think there's a good chance you'll stay in the new industry you're about to step into, then you may be better served finding a new job that's similar to what you're currently doing in a larger company or one with an easily recognizable brand name. That will lend you more credibility than working in a relatively unknown, small company. That was one of the reasons I chose to apply at Amazon: It is such a well-known company name that it would build credibility for my career path.

Something else to consider is the learning structure a company is able to provide. This is especially important if the particular job you're going for is one that will provide the opportunity to build your professional muscles. It may be difficult to research what that structure will be like in potential companies, but usually the more established a company is, the more robust their learning structures will be.

By being hired in an established company, you'll likely discover they have robust training and programs and policies already in place that will support you in the job you land and as you grow there. Whereas if you get a job with a startup, you'll often find yourself tossed into the fire and being tasked to figure things out. Granted, that doesn't happen all the time, but it is frequently the norm.

The intention of this book is to help you learn what you need to know in order to get in the door at your next job. But, always remember that wherever you are, you must maintain a perpetual habit of learning and expanding your skill set so that you can be successful in general.

Knowing what kind of learner you are will help with this step. I know I learn best when there is a strong structure and I have an assortment of documentation I can refer to. So for me, again, that means a well-established company that has the structure figured out and is well-regulated. If you're someone who learns best through trial by fire, then perhaps a startup or smaller company that's still figuring things out would be a good place for you.

In this case, to touch back on the idea of credibility for your next job, realize that not all startups are created equally. You can easily get name-brand credibility working for one that's a series B- or series C-funded company—they will have already been able to raise a couple million dollars in funding and will have some name recognition. Yet they may still be young enough for you to get that trial-by-fire education.

And finally, the last thing to think about is the mission of the company. Can you value and believe in what the company culture values and believes in? Does their mission resonate with you?

It's easy to wave this idea off. Most companies will say something about valuing their employees or their customers. Who can't support those? However, I promise it will benefit you to take a deeper look at those mission statements and ensure you can live up to what the company expects.

For example, Zappos is famous for its customer service. In alignment with their core value of delivering "WOW through service," when someone joined them, regardless of the position they were hired for, they were expected to spend a month answering calls from customers and work as a customer service rep before stepping into their actual job.[6] Everyone had to, including the executives. In fact, a new CFO was in the new hire group before mine and spent a full month answering incoming calls.

Customer service was taken so seriously there that on the holidays, everyone in the company (including C-level executives) had to work the

---

6   Zappos Stories, "Creating a Memorable Onboarding Experience | Zappos Stories," YouTube, 2020, https://www.youtube.com/watch?v=zD2SVwXMYHA

phone to support the customers. Not only that, but everyone had to appreciate the level of standard customer service so much that they could never show up later than one minute after their scheduled time for their shift—or they were at risk of being fired.

So you may be someone who says you are customer-oriented ... but are you *that* customer-focused? Could you happily remain in that culture? That's the kind of thing you'll need to consider as you review potential places to work. If you cannot believe in the company's vision or live and breathe in alignment with their purpose, then they may not be the best company for you.

Granted, all these points are guidelines. Only you will be able to weigh each factor according to how it will impact you. So if a company with a customer service demand like Zappos had a job that paid you a million dollars, versus working elsewhere for a fraction of that, you may find it in your best interest to suck up that first month just for the additional pay.

However, one thing that should always be weighed the most is the actual job: Is it something that interests you and gets you excited? Switching careers means you will be learning a new function or industry, and the way you will learn will be through the projects you complete and the actual job functions you'll do. If you absolutely hate those things, then any company, even an ideal one, should be ignored if that's the only kind of job they have.

I had applied to Amazon because, in addition to expanding my skill set and finances, I work best when I'm involved with things I use and can get excited about. Similarly, today, I work at Yelp selling its online reservation and waitlist solution to restaurants in a B2B2C role. Outside of work, I am someone who uses a service to make reservations at restaurants, so I resonate with what I do, and that drives the excitement I feel about my job.

So, as you think about how to prioritize the above points to choose companies, always keep in mind what resonates with you about particular jobs. Then, once you have a good idea which companies would make a good fit for you, you can complete the framework below to find the gaps between where you are and where you want to be. At that point, you'll be able to figure out what you need to learn to prepare for applying to (and successfully getting) the job.

The One-Page Framework

Once you've identified the ideal companies and positions you want to apply for, next up is to discover what you need to know or what skills you need to develop to make your job hunt successful. This framework will allow you to do just that. Ultimately, it will help you weed through all the information and suggestions from others about what you should do so you discover and focus on what will actually move the needle for you. This is the roadmap that will keep your focus and cut through the extraneous noise. As such, you'll get to make the switch quicker.

Name	
Company (Select one company only)	
Location (Select one location only)	
Job Title (Select one job title only)	
Skills I Have	1. 2. 3. 4. 5.
Skills I'm Missing	1. 2. 3. 4. 5.

Actions to Close the Gap	Currently Working On 1. Up Next 1. 2. Completed 1. 2.

It begins easily enough: Enter your name, the company you are looking at, and where you want to work. In *Company*, place only one company. The expectation here is that you do not choose any random company, but that you've gone through the above steps to narrow down companies you resonate with that have jobs you would find interesting. Then the location is where you are willing to work if it is not a remote position.

We'll use an example of Steven Smith's job hunt to complete the framework.

Similar to my trajectory, Steven wanted to go from inventory in a shoe company to sales in an entertainment company.

Steven chose Sony as his company because he wanted to change both job functions and industries. Why? Because in his role at the time, Steven was an inventory planner at Vans. There, he was tasked with analyzing sales trends and writing demand forecasts that ensured the right level of inventory would be available in the stores at the right times.

Steven wasn't in love with his job anymore. Retail and logistics had lost the appeal they once had to him. Additionally, he realized he wanted to have more interaction with people. He also thought it would be more exciting if he had a job that paid him based on his productivity, not just for showing up from nine to five every day. But, he wanted to stay in L.A., where he lived.

After researching industries and potential companies within them that resonated with him, he decided to apply for a position as an account manager at Sony Entertainment. Thus, the top of his one-pager looked like this:

Name	Steven Smith
Company (Select one company only)	Sony
Location (Select one location only)	Los Angeles
Job title (Select one job title only)	Account Manager

Things start to get a little more complex when you look at the next grouping of cells: *Skills I Have* and *Skills I'm Missing.* To complete both parts, Steven found the job description for account manager at Sony and reviewed all the qualifications. Under *Skills I Have*, he listed those that he felt matched the ones listed on the job description: Microsoft Office was one because he knew Excel, Word, Outlook, and Teams. He was super organized in general, especially with his calendar. He had a track record of working independently. And, with his inventory planner job, he amassed a great deal of knowledge around merchandising. So he listed those.

Skills I Have	1. Expert in Microsoft Office 2. Strong ability to organize calendar 3. Ability to work independently without supervision. 4. Knowledge in merchandising

What Steven didn't list was all the skills he had that were not specifically mentioned in the job description. Sure, they would make him look like a well-rounded and multifaceted candidate, but this one-pager was not for any potential employer to see. This was only for Steven's use, to figure out what he needed to do to get the job he wanted.

In the next set of cells he listed what skills he did *not* possess from the job description. Direct-to-consumer (DTC) strategy was one of them. DTC means selling either in-person or online directly to the customers without using a middleman. For example, you can purchase Adidas shoes directly from adidas.com, and that would be a direct-to-consumer sale. But if you bought those shoes in Nordstrom or Finish Line, the retailer would be the middleman in that sale. DTC was an area where Steven had never worked before, so it went on the list. Same with brand management, sales experience, and venue partnership. Again, all these qualifications came directly from the job description.

Steven was very honest with himself: Even if he felt he *could* do something already, that didn't matter. He didn't possess the specific skill set or knowledge base, so he entered those things under *Skills I'm Missing*.

Skills I'm Missing	
	1. D2C strategy
	2. Understand Shopify platform
	3. Brand management
	4. Sales experience
	5. Venue partnership

Completing the skills sections will be a bit of a gut check for you. As you go through the job description and learn about the different companies, you'll notice whether what will be expected of you will resonate with your why.

Going into this process, you may have had an idea of what it would be like to work in a certain capacity at a particular company, but when reviewing the skills, let yourself thoroughly think through them. Don't ignore signs suggesting you might not like to do something or that large parts of the job would not appeal to you. If you pay attention to them, you may just discover that what you thought could be your dream job is quite the opposite.

As soon as you recognize this, don't go forward with the framework. Go back to your list of companies, find a new position, and start the process over. Rinse and repeat until you are really clued in as to what your dream job might really be.

So far, all the boxes on the framework are filled in, and that's it. You leave them alone after that. In the last box, though, you'll be moving things down as you complete them. In this section, you'll choose one missing skill at a time and list it under *Currently Working On*. Then, you'll list the ways you will acquire that skill.

After you complete what's necessary, you'll move the missing skill to the completed list.

Of course, knowing where to start may be the tricky part here. Granted, if something is mentioned as a required qualification for a job, then each one could be seen as a good starting point. However, if you know nothing about the position or industry, maybe reading a book that introduces you to it is the best place to start. That will begin teaching you the language you'll need to learn. It may also point you to your next step.

Other options include attending industry conferences, local meetups for either the job function or industry (or both), industry events like the San Francisco tech week, and even online forums and articles.

Below, you can see that Steven leveraged Coursera, an online learning platform to learn about DTC business. He then went on to get a certification in Shopify foundations. He's currently working on one of his Skills Missing, sales experience, by reading a book, *The Challenger Sale*. To get further help on that, he's planning to attend a sales negotiation seminar. Then, to build out his skill set for the remaining two missing skills, he intends to take a brand-building class on LinkedIn Learning, and he has information interviews on tap with venue operators.

Actions to Close the Gap	**Currently Working On** 1. Reading *The Challenger Sale* **Up Next** 1. Sales negotiation seminar 2. LinkedIn learning: brand building course 3. Information interviews with venue operators **Completed** 1. Coursera: DTC business 2. Shopify: Shopify foundations certification

By sticking to the framework, Steven can stay focused on what he needs to do specifically to fulfill the requirements of the job qualifications. So if, in passing, someone tells him he should research social media as a sales medium, he doesn't get distracted. He might think that it makes sense, but when he refers back to his framework, he'll notice there's no mention of social media. In this way, he doesn't waste time on something that *could* be helpful, instead of focusing on what *will* be helpful.

Prioritizing like this is also a great reason to do some networking and seek help from a mentor. If you have someone who knows what the company or job position is like in your corner, you could let them know you've identified five things you need to work on, then ask them what they think would be the most beneficial order to learn them. A mentor can also provide good resources or projects for you to use or study. They can look at your gaps and tell you how they would close them—or even what they *did* to close them when they were in your position.

An added benefit of the framework is that it serves as more than just an anchor to help you stay focused on what you need to do to land the job you want. By doing what's necessary to gain the skills and qualifications you need, you will realize that the expectation is not to get to 100 percent fluency in the language required by that company or industry.

That said, remember that hiring managers will always find ways to challenge you and poke holes in your answers. As someone who sits on the opposite side of the table from candidates, I can tell you that one of the things I do is challenge them on the holes I see on their resume. I do that because I need to be sure they *can* do the job they're applying for when (if) I hire them.

The framework helps you to prepare for this. By completing the framework and following through on developing his missing skills, when Steven is asked about his lack of Shopify experience, he can reply with, "I received a certification in Shopify from that company." This will help the interviewer feel better about Steven's ability to do the job.

Following through on developing the missing skills is another way you might discover that your dream job may actually be a nightmare. Things may feel right and resonate with you when you initially review the job qualifications. But that resonance may shift into friction over the next six to 12 months you spend trying to fill in the skill gaps.

You have ample opportunity to discover that the job might not quite be what you're looking for. That's valuable information, because knowing that means you can start in a new direction without being bogged down by new job responsibilities.

By completing the framework, you build a foundation that will help you land your dream job—whether it's a job stepping stone or the actual one. It will help you stay focused on controlling what you can control, and it will help you be better prepared in an interview.

20/20 Hindsight

I didn't have this framework when I applied at Amazon. I had done the first part, though. I had figured out I wanted to apply at Amazon and I knew the job that I wanted. That process took me only a few hours because I already knew, geographically, where I wanted to be and what job function I wanted to do. And I knew the industry.

After I figured that out, I let it sit overnight. In fact, I let it sit for two days before I reviewed my ideas again. By doing that, I gave myself the mental and emotional distance to look at it with a fresh perspective.

However, because I didn't have the rest of the framework completed (or even invented at that point), I didn't know I wasn't really a viable candidate for the job.

If I had done this prior to applying for the Amazon position (really any position), I would have been better focused and able to prepare myself well enough that a job offer could have been made. Equally important: I would have saved myself so much time!

While I didn't get that job, I did get a job at Yelp, which was ultimately the destination I was aiming for. And it was a very straightforward process that went well and smoothly: I was offered the job right away. However, it only went so smoothly because of everything I'd learned over the years from the mistakes I'd made along the way. I got to my desired destination, and not someplace off the beaten path, because I was anchored in my why and had fully explored the skills and structure required of my dream job.

That's not to say I didn't try hard for the position. It just means I was ready to do the work required, which, in that case, meant accepting an interview over Christmas! I was on vacation in Park City, Utah, with my family. Instead of being outside snowboarding and skiing with my niece and nephew, I was inside, preparing for my interview, even on Christmas Day. If you really want the job, if it truly fulfills your why, you will want to make the sacrifice, as I did.

Perhaps what's most exciting is that the framework is all you really need. Consider the Pareto Principle—also known as the 80/20 rule—which suggests that 80 percent of a farmer's yield or profit typically comes from only 20 percent of their crops. If you apply the concept here, you can consider the framework to be the 20 percent that does the heavy lifting. Completing it will result in 80 percent of your impact, increasing your odds of going to 10 interviews and landing at least one job!

The goal of this book is summed up in this one framework: Let it be the anchor for you as you make your transition to a new position, function, or industry. The remaining chapters will support you after you complete the framework. They are full of hints, tips, and tricks that will help you succeed in your job transition.

CHAPTER 8

REVISITING YOUR WHY

During my transition from Mattel to Yelp, one of the companies I was interested in was SpaceX. I did fairly well with my interviews with them and made it all the way to the final round. They wound up offering the job to another candidate, someone who had both the function and industry expertise. They were able to plug and play him—slot him into the position without having to spend six months training him the way they would with me.

However, he turned down the position. So the recruiter called and offered the job to me.

At first, I was over the moon: Yes! A marketing position in a major tech company!

Frankly, the job seemed perfect. I loved the industry. I find space exploration fascinating. And I could honestly say that every person I'd met who worked at the company was great. They were all brilliant, welcoming, and approachable. The hiring manager was amazing—I greatly admired the way she carried herself and the way she explained things in our short interactions. I was blown away by the person I'd be reporting to. And there was ice cream! Free ice cream 24/7 at SpaceX! Could the job get any better?

Yes, yes it could get better ... but not at SpaceX.

At first, the SpaceX position did seem like it was the perfect job that had everything I wanted. But when the rosy afterglow of the offer faded, I realized it wasn't truly in alignment with my why: I'd have to take a major pay cut if I accepted the position.

I sat on the decision for a week, trying to figure out a way to make it work. Ultimately, I just couldn't do it. I had to turn them down. If I accepted the job, I wouldn't be able to make the mortgage payment on my place. More income was a key component of why I wanted to make a career switch. If I hadn't done all the prework to figure out my why, I may have accepted the job, telling myself I'd figure out a way to make it work.

And then being stressed over how, exactly, to make that happen.

Being Sure

Salary requirements can make it easy to determine whether a job meets your why or not—either it's enough money or it's not. Unfortunately, making that decision isn't always so easy, because the facts don't always line up in such a crystal-clear way.

Sometimes, whether in the initial stages of looking at companies or in the final interview, it's hard to know whether the job is the right one for you at that moment. It's times like these when you need a backup plan to ensure the decisions you're making are in alignment with your why. One of the tricks up my sleeve for such times is something I learned from my dad.

Believe it or not, I can be a very indecisive person. Often, to help me battle that, I'll make a list of pros and cons. Then, I'll write a new list of pros and cons. And then I'll write *another* list of pros and cons. Sometimes that will work, but most of the time I get frustrated because the pros and cons seem to come out equal. When frustration hits, I think about the red envelopes my dad used to give me.

In accordance with tradition, every Chinese New Year, my parents would give my sisters and me a red envelope with a little bit of money in it. Out of tradition, my dad would also tuck in a letter with it. He would take advantage of the yearly cycle to share with me what he felt I had done well the previous year and suggest a few areas I could improve during the upcoming one.

One year, when I was in high school, he prompted me to do a little introspection. He wrote: "Think about where you want to go in life. What kind of lifestyle do you want? Then, think about what you can do today—every day—to help you get closer to that lifestyle."

After receiving that letter from my dad, I found myself studying a little harder and playing fewer video games because I realized, for my long-term vision of my life to come true, that's what would be required.

The same idea can be applied to anything in life: If you think about where you want to be, you can learn what to do to get there. While the SpaceX job offer seemed to fill part of my why—the ability to leave a legacy—it couldn't help me in the direction of ensuring my freedom and security. So, looking through that lens, it was clear I had to say, "No."

Again, I didn't really need Dad's exercise to make the decision. Money can be a clearly defined black-and-white matter. But there's more to life than money, right?

For example, a director at one of the companies where I worked had a conversation with me shortly before he left the company. He made great money, which is why he had stayed on for such a long time. But the job demands increasingly crept in on his family time, and they came with quite a bit of stress. He was so stressed that his health was impacted and began to deteriorate.

When he thought about the kind of life he truly wanted, he realized it was one where he didn't just have more time with his kids but where he'd be more present with them. He would also have more energy because he'd be less stressed. By looking at where he wanted to be versus where he actually was, he realized he was in the wrong position.

He had accepted the job much earlier in his life when the trade-off between money and quality time outside of work tipped the scales the opposite way. But he had reached a point where he cared less about the money and more about the quality time outside of work with his family, so he made a career switch.

Similarly, a friend of mine was in a trusted, high-level position where she made close to a million dollars annually. When she accepted that position, she did so thinking it was a great title and an equally great income in an industry where she felt comfortable. However, the demanding 16-hour days, often seven days a week, were tougher on her body than she'd anticipated. She started suffering health problems from pushing herself too much. When she stepped back to see where she was, she realized it wasn't where she wanted to be. Sure, the money was nice, especially because it helped pay for medical bills. But what she really wanted was to feel good, to have energy, to have more of a work/life balance. So once she realized where she needed to be, she understood she had to quit her job. She accepted a position that paid less than half of what she used to make, but she's healthy again—and happier.

Your Why Can Change

As you can see from the last two examples, your why might change as you grow and evolve throughout your career. And that probably makes sense: If you look back to see where you were when you were just starting out, you'll realize you're a different person with different priorities. Our priorities change. Our likes and dislikes change. So of course, our whys will change as we grow older.

So that you don't find yourself behind the eight ball, feeling stressed, or stuck in a job that perhaps was once a dream but is now a nightmare, one thing you can do is periodically take my father's red envelope suggestion. Spend some time seriously analyzing your life and asking, "Where do I want to be in three years? In five years? In 10 years?" And so on. Then evaluate if you're on the right path to get there.

Do you think you'll be starting a family, so you'll want to work less? Or maybe you want to work more to provide for them. Do you think you'll want to be at an elevated position but you're now realizing, based on the evidence around you, that you need more schooling? Maybe you're starting to feel like I did after being exposed to a new industry: that that's really where you want to be. The options are endless. The paths to make those options come to life are, too. But you won't know how to head out on a new path, or to figure out what you'll need on that journey, unless you make yourself sit down and review your why as well as your life's goals to see how you can keep them in alignment.

What's Next?

So, by now you are positioned to start looking for your next gig. You know what job function you want and what industry it is in, and you have an idea of how to shorten the gap to help you land there. The framework in Chapter 7 helped you figure out how to prioritize what actions to take and how to take them. Really, you're in a good position to start looking.

What hasn't been spoken about in depth yet is interviews. How to handle them, how to prepare for them, how to master them, and how to keep the stress over them at a minimum. Let's look at all of that next.

PART 3

HINTS AND TRICKS FOR INTERVIEWS

CHAPTER 9

INTERVIEW TACTICS

One of the best ways to do poorly in an interview is by going in thinking your past experience and schooling are enough for you to answer questions in a way that impresses the hiring team. As many of my stories told in this book have shown, how you structure a response, how you tackle a Q&A, and how you understand the way you're being measured all require pre-interview prep work. Here are a few things to consider as you prepare.

Do Not Underestimate the Q&A

You will almost always be given five to 10 minutes at the end of each interviewing session to ask questions. In my opinion, this is the time when the great ones separate themselves from the good ones.

An example of what I mean happened when I was hiring somebody for my team at Mattel. I was interviewing a man who was making an industry and function switch—he was coming from a creative position at a movie company to work in marketing at a toy company. His answers during the regular portion of the interview were not very strong, but during the Q&A, a switch flipped and he did a phenomenal job. This changed the outcome of the hiring decision.

It was a 30-minute interview, which means I easily should have been able to ask several questions. I only got through three of them with him.

And they were not hard questions. They were very typical ones you get during interviews, such as "Tell me about a time when you had a conflict on the team; how did you resolve that?" The problem was that his answers were not well structured or concise—frankly, he spoke way too much. He struggled to be clear. Even worse, we barely got through just three questions. By the time we got to the Q&A, I wasn't able to gauge his skill set or what his experience was like.

When our time was up, I just didn't think he was the right person for the job. However, I'm a believer that interviews are two-way events and that I, as the hiring manager, need to make sure the other side has the opportunity to learn about the role. It doesn't matter whether I think the interview went well, because maybe the candidate was having an off day when they were with me; perhaps they had the opposite experience with the rest of the hiring team. Besides, it's just the right thing to do: It gives the candidate a better understanding of the company. If it doesn't work out this time, maybe they'll discover this is a place that would fit them, so they try again later for a different position. So, I left 10 minutes for him to do the Q&A. It was, by far, the most impressive Q&A that I had ever sat in.

Not only did he do more work than any other candidate to prepare for that Q&A, he really thought through each question he asked and proved how well he had prepared for the interview. For example, with one of his questions, he was so strategic that he was able to link the question back to the strategy that our CEO had spoken about during our most recent earnings call. He also asked about my other team, bringing up something that was in a report on the company. Super impressive! He made apparent all the research he'd done, which proved to me that he really wanted the job.

Furthermore, all his questions demonstrated that he had taken the time to understand the business focus of everyone he spoke to on the hiring team. At the time, I was working in an area of the company that few people knew anything about. It was an online collector platform that offered an exclusive kind of subscription membership. Even within Mattel, many people don't know about the program—but this guy took the time to do the research, noticed the platform, self-discovered the model, and strategically asked me about it.

"I saw the disconnect about how the model just seems a little bit confusing for the first-time users," he started, and then he asked me my view of it. So, not only did he know about that business focus of mine, but he tailored his question with me to discuss it. Likewise, he proved he had done the same kind of research for the other people on the hiring team. In short, he showed us his business acumen by being able to strategically connect the dots between the research, the data, and the strategy that was publicly out there to a question targeted at each one of us. Brilliant!

He was so strong in his Q&A that it was a no-brainer. We offered him the job.

There is a caveat here. If he had brought that information into his interview questions, the Q&A wouldn't have been a saving grace. He would have been a shoo-in for the job. Regardless, the Q&A can be the make-or-break moment of your hiring process.

Be Concise, Clear, and Cohesive

Most likely when being interviewed, you will be asked some standard questions that are frequently asked on job interviews. ("Tell me about a time when you managed conflict between team members.") Other questions may surprise you as they seem unrelated to the job. ("How many tennis balls do you think would fill this room?") And still others will be based on what piqued the hiring manager's interest when they looked over your resume and cover letter. ("What was it like studying abroad in England?") Regardless of the question, the same rules for good writing also apply to providing good interview answers: Be concise, be clear, and be cohesive. And the best way to do that is to be prepared!

Often there are no right or wrong answers to the questions you'll be asked. What hiring managers are hoping to do is get you to clarify things so we can fully understand your experience and capability. If you cannot clearly express that, you'll leave us guessing, and you risk taking up all your interviewing time with just a few long answers. Here are some strategies to help you be more concise.

Consider Going in Reverse

A common mistake people make is they just talk too much—especially with the very first question, which is usually, "Tell me about yourself" or "Walk me through your resume." Those are the same questions, really. And the number one worst way to answer that is by telling your story from the very beginning—where you graduated from, why you have that particular degree, how you landed your first job, etc. Hiring managers realize everyone is unique, but they don't want a diary-like recap of your professional life. That takes a long time and doesn't necessarily provide for them what they want to know.

Instead, for those first opening questions, I suggest you try to provide a more concise answer by taking a reverse strategy. Start by focusing on your most relevant job, which for most people is their most recent one. Talk about what you can bring to the table *now*. Because that's what we want to know: What are the top skills, talents, knowledge, or experience you have that we can tap into now? What is the key thing about you that makes you perfect for the job? Then handwave over the rest.

For example, when I interviewed for my current job at Yelp, which is in marketing, I only had my product marketing experience in my role at Mattel. So, in my interview, I started there. I explained what marketing does at Mattel, what my role and responsibilities were there, and how I could bring that experience to Yelp. Then, with a wave of my hand, I said, "I also developed my analytical skills—data analysis and financial forecasting—when I was at Gap and Zappos." I pretty much summed up what I did in those nonmarketing positions that would also be required in the job I was applying for at Yelp. In that way, I was able to keep the answer down to two minutes and open up the opportunity for the hiring manager to ask me other questions. My answers were strategically anchoring, too, because they kept the focus on the primary value that I'd bring coming into the job, which invited the hiring managers to ask follow-up questions in those areas.

An added benefit of going in reverse is that it helps you use an economy of words, which keeps your answers short. Unless you're replying to a use-case question where you're working through a project, keep your answers under three minutes if you can, and certainly no longer than five.

Clarity Is King

Bob Iger, the legendary CEO of Disney, said, "A strategy is only as good as your ability to articulate it."[7] Meaning, be clear! You have to be able to talk with clarity; otherwise, the person on the other side of the hiring desk, who has never lived through your experience, will get lost in the extra words and will have trouble understanding what you're trying to tell them. And if they cannot understand you during an interview process, they will not feel confident you can do the work required. This comes back to risk again: By not being concise and clear, you don't reduce the risk that comes with hiring you.

As the example in the Q&A section above shows, when someone is unable to express themselves clearly, not only do they risk being misunderstood, but they also risk not getting called back for a second interview.

The STAR Method

Providing answers to questions in a well-organized, relevant, and logical manner might sound difficult, but there's actually a formula that can help with it. It's called the **STAR** method for **Situation, Task, Action, Results**.

---

7   Bob Iger, "Business Strategy and Leadership," MasterClass, accessed August 1, 2020, https://www.masterclass.com/classes/bob-iger-teaches-business-strategy-and-leadership.

The STAR method is great for behavioral questions: "Tell me about a time where you failed, and what did you learn? Tell me about a project that you're super proud of. Give me an example of when you had disagreement with your cross-functional partners and how you handled it." By using this method, you can concisely and clearly provide examples of your achievements and showcase how you problem-solved.

First, you describe the **situation** the question is asking about. You follow that up by explaining the **task** you were given in that situation and the goal you were aiming to reach. Then you talk about the **actions** you took to complete the task. Finally, you bring up the outcome—the **results**—you achieved and what you learned along the way.

For example, let's say in an interview you were told the company is focused on growth, and then they pitch a question to you to see how you've been instrumental in driving growth in the past. Your answer could be (hypothetically speaking): "In my previous position, we were the go-to for the widget product and had captured about 70 percent of the market share for it. So when the company wanted to grow, we felt we needed a new product to enter a new market." (That's the situation.) "It was assigned to me to figure out what that new product would be" (the task). "In market research, I discovered a new space to go after. So, I pitched an idea to leadership and was able to get funding, which allowed me to create a team." (That describes the actions you took.) "We were able to develop a new product in two years. The new product launched six months ago, and we've already hit three million in incremental revenue for the company" (the results).

Notice that it is all very high-level, which keeps your answers brief and focused on the main points. You can see how it's possible to provide just the core information and yet expose many of your job skills. The above answer told them that you know how to do market research, be innovative, build a team, manage a budget, and bring a new product to market. If the hiring manager wants to know more about certain aspects, they will ask for details about those things. Depending on what that particular hiring manager wants to know, they will zero in on that and ask for more targeted answers.

Again, the STAR method is best for behavioral questions. Case questions need an entirely different approach.

Case Questions

Everyone should expect case questions at some point in their job-pivoting journey. They will not be from the recruiter who does your first screening interview. Just like with the Uber laundry case question I shared earlier, you will start being asked these types of questions when you get beyond that initial interview and meet with the hiring manager and team. Basically, they give you a true opportunity to showcase how you think through a potential (or real-life) scenario and how clearly you are able to communicate your thought processes.

A pretty common or famous example of a case question is when the candidate is handed a pen and asked to sell it. Or you may be put in a time and place and asked, "Where do you think revenues will be in a year?"

One of the strategies I take with case questions is I'll show potential candidates a list of products recently launched by the company, describe the audience for those products, and then pose a problem and ask the candidate how they would solve it. Or, I'll ask them to pick a product and ask them how they'd promote it to the market.

Other case questions, as we'll explore further below, may ask you to imagine you're in an elevator with your CEO. If the CEO asks for our projections over the next year, how would you create an answer for them?

As you can see, case questions have a vague quality about them, which can make them difficult to answer. And it might go against everything you've been taught in your academic career, but there are no right or wrong answers with case questions. So instead of aiming for "the right" answer like on the SAT exam, aim for demonstrating your ability to be a critical thinker in clear and concise ways.

In fact, when most hiring managers ask case questions, they aren't looking for a specific answer. Instead, they want to see *how* you get to your answer.

They want to see your critical thinking skills, how you analyze situations, and how well you present your answer. They want to know if you have the ability to then strategically build on that analysis to give recommendations.

Your answers to case questions show them whether you can ask the right questions regarding the problem or situation you're facing. Can you analyze the information you receive from those questions? Can you take the information you just broke down in an analysis, find the pattern, and provide a recommendation?

An example of case questions comes from a friend of mine who works for a very large public company. One of his favorite questions to ask candidates now is, "Let's go back in time to late April 2020. The pandemic has set in; the country is pretty much shut down. You're on a Zoom call when your CEO asks if you think revenues will go up or down this year. What would you tell him?" To look at potential answers, let's say the company is a toy manufacturer.

One answer could be: "Revenue will be up because, according to the news, people are buying more toys for kids now that they're stuck at home. And we saw stock prices for the company go up as a result of all the online shopping." While that answer proves you did your homework researching the company's past performance, it does little to show your critical thinking abilities. So, you could say the answer was correct—in that it matched what happened historically—but it's not a good answer for the hiring manager.

A better answer would be something like: "I believe revenues will be down, because when I look at the global supply chains, fewer people are working, which means that there are not enough people to move the inventory. I'm guessing there will be a big backlog, whether that's in shipping or inventory or both. We might not have the people available to move the products to warehouses or retailers. Since stores can't sell inventory they don't have, they won't be selling the toys stuck in the backlog. Also, during times like these, people tend to stick to only buying essentials, and toys seldom fall into that category. Besides, so many toys are impulse buys that people like to touch and explore before they pull out a credit card for them.

With so many people afraid to touch things that others have touched, any in-store impulsive decisions will be hampered."

That answer shows you're doing some critical thinking—you understand what needs to happen in order for people to get access to and buy toys, and you're thinking about how that could be impacted by the pandemic. However, it could be even better. That was a good answer; let's look at how it could be great.

Great case question answers often begin with questions, because you need to better understand the situation. Frequently, as in this example, you are missing a lot of data points, so you need to learn them first before building your argument.

In the above scenario, you'd start by asking, "How much of your business is online versus retailer-driven?" Other good questions would be, "Are there also things that the retailers are doing that impact our business? Are they cutting back on marketing or buying less inventory?" "What's the situation with our factories? Do we own them, or do we partner with others? Are we still able to operate them?" "Are the issues with production global or geographically limited?" Because blockbuster movies often positively correlate with toy sales, another question to ask might be: "Are any major movies going to be released that could drive interest in particular lines of toys?"

By starting with questions to gather information and get a conversation going with the hiring manager, you prove you know what questions to ask to start breaking down the problem and how to gather the data required to do an analysis of a situation. Then you take the information you're provided, explain how you think it applies to the situation, and then provide your answer. For example: "Well, we know that online sales have been strong, offsetting the drop of in-store revenue. However, the sustainability of strong online sales is not probable because factory production has been significantly delayed due to the government's restrictions allowing only 25 percent of workers to return to work. A similar thing is happening in the shipping industry, which means the inventory cannot get to the stores and the warehouses, impacting online sales as well as in-store. So, I think we risk running out of inventory both online and in-store as we get into the Q4 holiday season, our biggest revenue-generating time of year. Additionally, the movie industry has also been impacted by the pandemic, and we don't have anything scheduled to come out this year to give us a boost in sales. So, in summary, I think revenues will be down for the year."

That is a great answer. Really, there was quite a bit of context missing from the original question asked, but by asking clarifying questions you can fill in the gaps to gather and analyze data, and then come up with a clear answer.

So, the key to answering case questions:

1. Ask the right questions to get you closer to an answer. You're gathering the necessary information to fill in what you don't know. Just two or three category questions will be enough to provide some data. Remember, you will want to keep your answer short. So try to focus on, at most, three different buckets of data.
2. Analyze the information you received.
3. Make a decision that is data-driven and backed up by your critical thinking on the answers.

Note that the quality of the answer doesn't include whether or not it was correct. Again, there are no right or wrong answers in terms of whether you made an accurate prediction or forecast. What matters is that you are clear, concise, and cohesive as you walk the hiring manager through your thought processes.

If you get a case during an interview, the hiring manager wants to see how you come up with solutions. Your experience will also be evidenced here. Because of the time limits on the interview, there is no expectation that the answer will be polished or will cover every possible scenario. In this situation, you are most likely alone with the hiring manager, who will also be the one to provide follow-up questions.

If you get the case question 24 to 48 hours ahead of time, things will be a little different. You will still need to prove your thinking and reasoning skills as well as evidence you experience, but these often take the form of a presentation you give to a panel that consists of the hiring manager and others on the hiring team.

Your answer to these kinds of case questions will need to be well-thought-out, as deeper expectations will be placed on you. You will still not be expected to cover every possible scenario, but you will need to be prepared to provide more than one possible perspective. Also, you'll be asked follow-up questions by multiple stakeholders with different points of view to test how well you thought through your answers and how you handle dealing with a cross-functional team.

Now that you know how to handle being in the interview itself, let's look at things outside of the interview, so you can do an even better job preparing to sit across from an interviewer.

CHAPTER 10

PREPARING FOR INTERVIEWS

As many of my personal stories have shown, I spent quite a bit of time outside of my interviews getting ready for them. The most impactful strategies that set me up to perpetually keep doing better on my interviews were: Getting feedback, being aware of who might hear me, thinking about my career switching in steps, and using good negotiating techniques.

Get Feedback

Always ask interviewers for feedback after you receive a rejection—and even when you receive an offer. This might take a lot of courage, but drumming it up will pay off in the long run.

When I interviewed with DoorDash, I made it very far along in the process. I think there were six rounds of interviews, and I made it to the fifth before they rejected me. Ouch. With the sting of that still hurting, I reached out to the hiring manager for feedback. He was wonderful. He walked me through everything—not just his perspective, but the whole hiring team's. He pointed out some things I did very well and some things where I needed improvement. He also discussed with me a few other concepts he thought I should keep in mind. He then thanked me for the time I put into preparing for the interview.

All in all, it was a very positive and even empowering conversation that, yes, helped me prepare better for the next interview. In fact, what he did was explain to me that I needed to do a better job of connecting the dots since I was coming from a different industry. He showed me how I hadn't been able to prove I'd filled in a gap.

The best person to provide feedback is the last one you interviewed with; however, the rule of thumb is to first contact the recruiter. Only reach out to someone above them if you've been given explicit permission to do so (as was my case with DoorDash) or if you are passed on to them directly.

Keep in mind that sometimes a recruiter or hiring manager may not be able to provide feedback because of company policies or because they are strapped for time and just don't have the bandwidth. But, for the most part, they want everyone to succeed, so they will often be happy to talk to you if they can.

The Walls Have Ears

With so many elements being outside your control, you want to be careful with those that are—which includes what you say to others. Remember the six degrees of separation example? Sophie landed her VP job because so many people spoke positively about her. Those kinds of connections don't just spread what's positive about people—they can also spread the negative. You can't control what someone reports to potential employers. If you provide the fodder by badmouthing a company or industry, they will do with it what they will.

I get how easy it can be to vent sometimes—particularly after a rejection or when feeling stressed about an upcoming interview. But walls do have ears, sometimes. A recruiter I know recently told me a man at the table next to her at a restaurant was loudly complaining about a company he was interviewing with—a company that she was recruiting for! That can happen anywhere. So control what you say and when you say it.

So many people are connected these days, and you never know who might be connected to you via a mutual acquaintance—or who might remember you from two jobs ago as you move from position to position.

Making the Switch in Steps

Depending on your goal, you might benefit by thinking about making your career switch in a series of multiple steps. Whether it's switching functions to work at a major brand to give yourself some "street cred," or by starting at a lower level and working your way up, you can take a stepping-stone approach to getting to your dream job.

The first, gaining street cred, happened to me somewhat by accident. It wasn't anything I had planned for, but something I learned in hindsight. It started the first time I interviewed at Mattel. At the time I was looking for an internship position while I was still in business school. The internship would be my first marketing position.

I went through the normal application process, which included several rounds of interviews, and had made it all the way to a final interview with the VP of marketing. I was pumped to be in the running for a marketing job. As I went through the interviews, I was well prepared, so I felt confident … until that last interview.

I was asked questions I just wasn't prepared for. As I responded, I realized I didn't even understand the words coming out of my mouth—so I was certain the interviewer didn't. And the look on his face confirmed it. He was very polite and professional as he ended the interview, but I walked away thinking I'd never hear from them again.

Fast-forward a couple of weeks, when I got a call to see if I was still interested in the internship. Imagine my surprise! Of course I was, though I did wonder if they'd called the wrong person by mistake.

I wound up landing on that VP's team and worked on part of his portfolio. We got to know each other pretty well, so at the end of my summer internship, when he asked to speak to me before I left, I drummed up the courage to ask him for some feedback.

"I didn't feel like I did well in my interview with you," I told him. "There were questions that I felt like I bombed. I was wondering if you could give me some feedback."

He had the grace to ignore my mistakes. "At the end of the day," he said, "when I looked at your resume, I saw that you had already worked at Zappos, an Amazon company, and Gap. Those two companies are heavy hitters. I figured if you could cut it with them, there was a good chance you could cut it with us."

A couple of weeks after that conversation, I received a call from the chief brand officer of the company asking me if I'd like to return to Mattel as a full-time employee. It still wasn't my dream job—remember, I was hoping to go into entertainment or tech. However, yes, I wanted the job with Mattel. I knew I'd be able to learn much more about marketing while there, which would help me one day land that position in an entertainment company.

For each new position, I had to prepare and negotiate, which brings me to my final tip: how to negotiate.

Negotiations

A caveat is needed here: I'm not an expert on negotiating and have never claimed to be one. There are many good books already written on negotiations if you want a deeper dive. What I'm trying to offer here is my take on negotiations.

As mentioned in Chapter 4, hiring managers go through a lot of work to get your position approved. So they have an incentive to get you to sign on the dotted line—they don't want to have to start the process all over again if you don't take the offered job. That would mean another three months of juggling their daily responsibilities while they find, vet, and interview another candidate.

You can probably understand, then, why they really appreciate it when you're up-front about things like salary expectations or make-or-break deals. As a candidate for SpaceX, I totally failed to do that. Because money was important to me, I should have discussed it up-front, very early in the interviewing process. But I was so fascinated by SpaceX while communicating with them that I never really got a clear answer on what the salary would be until I found myself in the position of having to turn the company down. If I'd known for sure at the beginning, I wouldn't have wasted anyone's time with interviews.

By being up-front about your salary, you will save time (yours and the hiring company's), and you will also let the hiring manager know whether you have realistic expectations for the position. You should have done some research to know what the position would pay and be within the ballpark of a fair range when you discussed it with HR or the hiring manager during the early interview process.

This concept goes beyond salary, though. It can include signing bonuses, equity, or any other payouts. It also includes negotiating your start date and amount of paid time off. Be clear about what you want, and don't wait until the last minute to communicate it. In fact, it's preferable to discuss your compensation up-front in a clear and concise manner. For example, if the total compensation package is most important to you, provide your expectations for that. Other people, in comparison, may need to express their desire for a certain base salary.

A key thing to remember is that you're just being open and honest when you're being up-front about your compensation expectations—this is not the point of negotiations. You are having a two-minute conversation where the hiring side can say "yes" or "no" regarding whether they can offer what you want. As far as other desirables, like start date, paid time off, etc., save that for the negotiations after you are given an offer.

In other words:

Step 1: Express your expectations regarding compensation and ask what their usual pay is for the position. The goal in this initial conversation is to be sure you are both playing in the same ballpark. Prioritize what you really want and need, double-check that you're thinking in alignment with the industry norms, and then ask with clarity. The worst that can happen is they say "No," and both parties have saved time by knowing they are not a fit.

Step 2: Once you receive an offer, tell them the top one or two things that are most important to you. Is it better pay? Year-end bonus? At this point, the hiring manager will be making the case for you with leadership and the compensation team.

Step 3: If they give you what you want, then great! If they cannot, then that's when you can start negotiating the secondary things you want like PTO, professional development funds, start date, etc.

Be aware that when you ask, you must be realistic. Realize the hiring manager is the person who will be overseeing your training during your probationary period. They will evaluate you and decide what projects you'll be working on. They have a lot of say over what your career within the company will be like. So why make things rough on them from the outset by demanding potentially more than the job can bear?

Your hiring manager wants you to be happy with the job. So, if you go in with reasonable expectations, and they are excited because they think you are the ideal candidate, they will fight for you. If you make it hard for them to win that fight, or seem too demanding, even if you get what you want, you may not be starting with your best foot forward.

CONCLUSION

ROME WASN'T BUILT IN A DAY

When I was getting ready for college, my dad gave me a book in Chinese. Translated, the title is *Stanford's Silver Bullet: School. Workplace. Love. And Life's Secret Weapon.*[8] I wasn't going to Stanford, nor was I about to enter graduate school, but my dad realized the book was full of life lessons told through the author's personal experience in grad school. He thought those lessons could be helpful to me, and they were.

It is my wish that this book does something similar for you as you stand at the crossroads of a career pivot. I've found making a career switch can be one of the most powerful and exciting things to do, not just with your career, but with your life. And I truly hope you find similar results, though it may take some time.

As a manager I highly respect here at Yelp says, "Nobody starts in world-class." That line is especially relevant with career switches—you never start at the world-class level. But you also won't get to world-class if you never start, nor if you don't have the discipline to stick with the process.

It takes time to learn how to be good at interview questions. It takes time to understand a company or industry well enough to bridge your language or learning gaps. And when you're making a career switch while currently employed, that's a lot to handle. You can't just cram an eight-hour class into one hour and expect to achieve a great outcome. You might have to spread

---

8   Wen Hua Wang. *Stanford's Silver Bullet.* Taipei: China Times Publishing Company, 2005

that eight-hour class over a week or two, which is where patience and, again, discipline come in. You must learn to pace yourself so you don't burn out.

The first half of this book was really devoted to setting your expectations and creating the right mindset around what will be involved in making a switch. You won't know exactly what you'll need to do until you get started. Only then will you truly understand what's ahead of you and be able to refine what you need to do, fitting it into your day in a way that won't exact a mental or physical toll. So, be kind to yourself. Trust the process. Keep up the discipline and remember: You might not be able to start in world-class, but you can always finish there.

Clearly, it can be quite the learning experience as you do whatever you need to in order to bridge the gap. Whether you become educated with the language of an industry or about how different companies use various strategies to problem-solve, everything you learn only makes you a more well-rounded individual.

The tools that you read about here can also be applied throughout other areas of your life. Learning to keep your ego out of the way—to build healthy, equally supportive relationships—and developing the habit of listening to your body will benefit you in multiple ways. In addition, the tools to be introspective as you evaluate where you want to go in your career can also be applied to your lifestyle choices, hobbies, relationships, and any kind of planning for your future.

Always remember, you control your destiny—whether you do it deliberately by taking action or passively by letting things happen to you. I suggest you take control.

Control Your Destiny

There's a saying I heard during business school that I really like: "Don't stop until you sign your offer." For me, that means you keep hunting for positions; continue researching companies and industries; keep rehearsing interview answers; and don't stop getting, analyzing, and integrating feedback until you are completing your new-hire paperwork for your next job.

Career switching is like driving: If you take your foot off the gas, then you're trusting gravity and physics to get you to where you want to go. Coasting along, hoping the momentum you had in the past will carry you through, will not get you far. As I learned from an executive at Mattel, *hope* is not a strategy. You must continually keep your foot on the gas and actively steer to get to your desired destination.

I'm not saying you shouldn't take breaks—you don't want to push yourself to exhaustion or damage your body from stress. It can be a very long journey, and sometimes taking breaks is actually part of taking control. You're managing your physical and mental resources in an appropriate way that will help you continue.

The point is: You must continue. The best control you can exert is to take action. Do everything you can, and even if you don't get the outcome you want, at least you won't have any regrets as you continue on. If you leave it to chance, if you put in some effort and then take your foot off the job-hunting gas indefinitely, then you leave your future at risk.

So I hope you take full advantage of everything you learn in this book, even beyond just job hunting. Whether you learn something from my personal stories or from any of the other pieces of advice I've shared, I hope you find this book to be a valuable resource, something you can refer back to again and again.

ABOUT THE AUTHOR

Mike was born in Taipei, Taiwan, and moved to the United States at the age of 13 with a limited grasp of the English language. As an adult, Mike wore multiple hats for over a decade, working to drive business growth for multiple billion-dollar-plus companies across the retail and technology space. He earned his MBA from the University of Southern California, where he continues to be involved as an alumnus and in helping current students find their career paths. Mike also holds a dual degree in Economics and Communications from the University of California, San Diego. He lives in Southern California and spends much of his free time soaking up the sunshine and the ocean breeze at the beach.

You can learn more about Mike at www.pioneeryourpivot.com.